Pamphlets for the Faithful

Pamphlets for the Faithful

by Fr Willie Doyle, SJ

THE CENACLE PRESS
AT SILVERSTREAM PRIORY

This collection is based upon the pamphlets of Fr William
Doyle, SJ, and published by The Irish Messenger as follows:
Retreats for Men and Boys (1909)
Vocations (1913)
Rubrics of the Mass (1914)
Shall I Be a Priest? (1915)
Scruples and Their Treatment (posthumously)

This edition published
© 2023 by Silverstream Priory.

The Cenacle Press at Silverstream Priory
Silverstream Priory
Stamullen, County Meath, K32 T189, Ireland
www.cenaclepress.com

ppr 978-1-915544-84-1

Book design by Nora Malone
Cover design by Silverstream Priory

Contents

Introduction

One of the vital concerns for Fr Willie Doyle in his life as a Christian and a priest was holiness, not only seeking it for himself, but encouraging it and supporting it in those he served. The five pamphlets he authored, his only published works, have at their heart, sanctification through the service and worship of God. Two of these deal with vocations, responding to God's call to the life of consecration and service in the Church; one promotes the spiritual life among the laity through retreats; another offers priests assistance in the celebration of Holy Mass; and the last, published after his death, deals with scruples, a serious barrier to progress in holiness.

Born into a comfortable middle-class family in Dalkey, Co. Dublin, Willie inherited a rather bourgeois way of life, but, like his exact contemporary and spiritual soulmate, St Thérèse of Lisieux, his early years were marked by a faith that was both contemplative and pragmatic: family prayer and spiritual reading augmented by charitable works and awareness of the needs of others. When he embraced the religious life, he did so out of love for Christ and for others, centring his consecrated life and priesthood on an act of martyrdom offered to Christ through the hands of Our Lady as he prepared to take his first vows in 1893. That martyrdom was first to be manifested in a life of sacrifice and service and then, he hoped, by God's grace and through the prayers of Mary, consummated in his dying a Jesuit martyr. His death on the battlefield at Passchendaele in Belgium during World War I, on 16 August 1917, as he was trying to save two wounded soldiers, was the martyrdom he desired: offering his life for Christ and his neighbour. In essence, this was the nature of Willie Doyle's holiness.

For Willie, holiness was simply loving God and living in God. Every moment of every day, every action, every word could be embraced and offered for the love of God. Given his natural generosity, Willie was not inclined to refuse anything to God, but he often struggled like the rest of us to be completely open at times. Thanks to a natural gift of self-awareness and St Ignatius' Spiritual Exercises which he loved, Willie was aware of his weaknesses and the barrier they could construct between him and God and God's will for him; he knew that if he was to make any progress in the spiritual life, he had to battle against those weaknesses. The fruit of this struggle was not just personal holiness, but a deep wisdom which helped him guide others in their spiritual lives. Though tough on himself, he was gentle with others, indeed his advice mirrored that of St Thérèse's Little Way, advising people to see in the ordinary trials of life all the penance they needed to assist their sanctification. As a man who was wrapped in prayer himself, he urged others to seek out the Lord in prayer and adoration, to make their home in the Heart of Jesus and to allow him to woo them as does the Lover the Beloved in the *Song of Songs*.

INTRODUCTION

We may understand this as the context and background to Willie's writings. His two pamphlets on vocations seek to help and advise those discerning a vocation to the priesthood and religious life, understanding that this is an invitation to a life centred on Christ, on selfless service of the Church and evangelical perfection. Initially, Willie did not want to write these pamphlets, but as he had been inspired in his discernment by St Alphonsus Liguori's *Instructions and Considerations on the Religious State*, he felt that young people needed a similar work to benefit their discernment. St Alphonsus' work, however, was quite a tome which few seemed inclined to read, and as no one had to date produced a simpler book, Willie embraced the task himself. The pamphlets are of their time in terms of language and expression, but their core message is timeless as Willie is eminently practical in his advice. He prefaces *Vocations* (1913) with a quotation from Psalm 35, 'Blessed are they that dwell in Thy house, O Lord', reminding his reader that to embrace a vocation to priesthood or religious life is to enter into the household of God as stewards and servants, and that Christ has called the individual to follow *him*. Even if Willie offers a rather forbidding quotation from St John Henry Newman to follow the quotation from the psalms, he emphasises that responding to a vocation is a free choice and for those who make it, God will provide the graces necessary to respond. In his work *Shall I Be a Priest?* (1915), very much a sequel to *Vocations*, though couched in the somewhat sentimental language of his time, Willie explores the priestly vocation in its various aspects, from the priesthood of Aaron to priesthood of Jesus, the celebration of the sacraments, priestly holiness, and aids to the discernment of a priestly vocation. These pamphlets sold well even during his short life, hundreds of thousands of copies reaching men and women all over the world, helping thousands make the decision to offer their lives to God for service in the Church.

Closely related to his pamphlet on the priesthood, *Synopsis of the Rubrics and Ceremonies of Holy Mass* (1914) is a concise guide for priests on how to offer the Mass. Willie's own devotion to the Mass was unparalleled and his war letters, written to his father from the Front during his military service (1915-1917), detail the often difficult circumstances in which he took pains not only to offer Mass but to do so with reverence and devotion, in the ruins of bombed churches, in trenches, surrounded by the bodies of the dead, for communities of religious sisters fearful that a shell could fall on their chapel at any moment. These experiences deepened Willie's love of the Mass and without doubt confirms the little labour of love this pamphlet was. Too often priests were poorly instructed in how to offer Mass reverently and well, some fell victim to speedy celebrations or were frequently distracted. Willie's little 'rubrical' is not offered as an obsessional manual, but rather one to help the priest focus on what he is doing when he offers Mass and deepen his recollection. Regardless of which form of the Mass priests offer, this little pamphlet can be useful to deepen their Eucharistic awareness and spirituality.

One of Willie's ardent tasks was that of promoting retreats among working men. He was among the pioneers of such a movement in Europe at the turn of the 20th century. Experiments in France and Belgium had proved successful and having studied them Willie composed *Retreats for Men and Boys: Why Not in Ireland?* in 1909; it was his first pamphlet. While not excluding women from this spiritual exercise, Willie was acutely aware of how men can neglect religious observance and how working men in particular had so few opportunities to take time apart to pray and grow in their faith. Aware of the times in which he lived, and of various ideologies which were quickly becoming a challenge to Christianity, Willie saw the potential of a lay apostolate in the world and the workplace to evangelise and meet those challenges. His pamphlet was part of his efforts to set up a retreat house for working men in Ireland; he was one of a number of priests involved in this task, and he had some success, giving a retreat at the Foxford Mills for its workers in 1915 and acquiring a premises in Rathfarnham Castle in Dublin as a more permanent base. His efforts came to end, however, following the centre's being burnt down by suffragettes. It fell to others after his death to continue the work. Holiness, Willie understood and taught, was not the preserve of priests and religious; every Christian was called to become holy, and the Church had to provide every means necessary to help ordinary men and women to achieve this holiness; he understood that providing retreats for the laity was a vital part of the Church's mission.

As an experienced guide of souls, Willie was aware of the challenges people faced in the spiritual life as they sought holiness, chief among them scruples. Quite apart from being an affliction experienced by people in every place and time, Ireland at the beginning of the 20th century was infested with Jansenism, which Willie deplored, and this bred excessive spiritual problems, scruples foremost among them. Though he never saw it in print, *Scruples and their Treatment* is his attempt to offer a rational and effective means to deal with the affliction. Drawing on a work by

Father R. P Dupois, Willie's work is not a slavish reproduction of Dupois's ideas; rather he draws on his own experience in dealing with the problem. The pamphlet is written in a straightforward, rational style and is very practical. There is also no room for any scrupulosity in its ideas and advice—Willie was well aware of the cracks and fissures in which scruples can lurk in the minds of those suffering from them.

Fr Willie Doyle's reputation for holiness has endured since his death in 1917. The outpouring of devotion to him in the decades after his death continues to this day as new generations discover his life, his vibrant personality, his heroism and his writings. The various biographies written over the years reproduce his private writings – his letters and thoughts as preserved in spiritual diaries and notes, which he wanted destroyed following his death; these five pamphlets are the works he intentionally wrote to assist souls in their spiritual lives. In a sense, this is the legacy Willie wanted to leave behind, so they are precious for that reason alone, although his legacy is far greater in terms of his life and holiness. The republication of these pamphlets, together in one volume for the first time, is indeed welcome not only for the matters they deal with, but perhaps even more for the insights they give us into a man whom many hope will be declared a saint one day; a man whose vibrant life and personality is as accessible and endearing to us now as it was to those who knew him in life.

—Fr John Hogan, OCDS
Diocesan Postulator for the Cause of
the Servant of God, Fr Willie Doyle, SJ

Retreats for Men and Boys

Why Not in Ireland?

Nihil obstat: Gulielmus Henry, S.J., *Cens. Theol. Dep.*

Imprimi potest: † Eduardus, *Archiep.*
Dublinen., Hiberniae Primas

Retreats for Workingmen
Their Scope and Organization

"A work providential among all others."

—Pius X

Origin

The year 1882 saw the commencement, in the north of France, of a work which has been singularly blessed by God. For many years small groups of gentlemen had been in the habit of annually devoting three days, in some religious house, to prayer and recollection, making what is commonly known as a "Retreat."

A French Jesuit, Père Henry, knowing the marvellous power of the Spiritual Exercises of St. Ignatius for the sanctification of souls, conceived the bold idea of bringing the labouring classes under their influence, of establishing "Retreats for Workmen."

The proposal met with some little encouragement and plenty of ridicule. It was an Utopian idea, impossible to achieve, especially in the industrial centres of northern France, among the miners, artisans and mechanics of the big towns—men not over-given to piety, and who could not find time even for their Paschal duty. Retreats for Workmen! To expect these uneducated toilers to spend three whole days in solitude and silence, thinking only of God and their soul, praying, meditating—that was all very well for monks and religious, but for men of the world impossible! Moreover, such a scheme required both time and money; where could one find workingmen with an over-abundance of both or the willingness to part with either?

When God wants a work done human difficulties are no obstacle. A house was hired near Lille, modestly furnished, and the first retreat for workingmen announced for the 27th of May. Would they come? Twenty responded to the appeal, with no little diffidence and fear of the unknown before them. At the end of the three days every heart was won and all pledged themselves to try and induce their comrades to follow their example, and find within the walls of the Château Blanc the happiness given by a well-made retreat.

The success of the project was assured. Before the end of 1882 eleven more retreats had been given to two hundred and ten men; in the following year 340 workers from the neighbouring towns made the "Exercises."

In ten years' time seven other houses were opened in various parts of France—at Amiens, Paris, Reims, Bordeaux—where, year after year, hundreds of men have learned in the holy solitude of the retreat that life has a nobler end than the mere seeking for wealth or pleasure; that the true dignity of man consists in the loyal service of his Creator and not slavery to his passions.

The Work in Belgium

Since the foundation of "Retreats for Workmen" Belgian Catholics had followed the progress and rapid extension of the work with keen interest. At the suggestion of Mgr. Doutreloux, Bishop of Liège, Père Lechien, S.J., during the vacation of 1891, assembled eighty-six workmen at the Jesuit College of Charleroi for a three days' retreat. The result was so consoling, the good done so evident, it was resolved to open at once at Fayt-lez-Manage, between Mons and Charleroi, a house devoted entirely to retreats for workingmen. What France could do for her sons Belgium could and would do also.

At the outset many difficulties were encountered; opposition and discouragement from those who preferred to support existing social works rather than encourage new ones. Progress was slow, but none the less certain. In four years 1,498 men had spent three days in the solitude of Fayt. The work was firmly established, and in rapid succession houses of retreat were built at Ghent, Arlon, Lierre, Liège, and Alken.

In these six houses, almost every week, sometimes twice in the same week, a retreat is given to groups of from thirty to sixty exercitants.

A glance at the figures for one year—1908 (January to December)—will convey some idea how successful the undertaking has been, and the enormous good effected:—

House	Retreats	Exercitants
Fayt	48	2,366
Ghent	36	1,314

House	Retreats	Exercitants
Arlon	34	1,300
Lierre	37	1,692
Xhovémont	43	1,720
Alken	34	1,261
Tronchiennes	11	600
Total	243	10,253

The following table gives the numbers for each house since its foundation:—

House	Retreats	Exercitants
Fayt (1891-1908)	650	26,087
Ghent (1894-1908)	500	16,136
Arlon (1896-1908)	275	9,445
Lierre (1899-1908)	457	19,377
Xhovémont (1901-1908)	326	12,205

House	Retreats	Exercitants
Alken (1905-1908)	130	4,646
Tronchiennes	255	16,000
Total	2,593	103,896

The Belgian women have not been slow to realize the advantages of a retreat. Fifteen houses have already been opened by different congregations of nuns, and retreats given last year to nearly 15,000 working girls and mill hands.

Holland and England

Holland was now to test the efficacy of what the present saintly Pontiff calls "a work providential among all others." In May, 1906, the first band of Dutch exercitants—fifty men from the works at Maestricht—left for the newly-erected retreat house at Xhové-mont, Liège, and returned transformed. Within a few months 900 more from various parts of Holland had followed their example. The experiment, successful from the start, had proved that Holland was ready for the sowing of the good seed which had produced such abundant fruit in France and Belgium. A committee of zealous, influential laymen, including several members of both Chambers, was formed for the erection of a house of retreats. Venloo, situated in the north of Limburg, close to the German frontier, was chosen as the site, and a large building, containing a chapel, dining hall, library, etc., with rooms for seventy men, was solemnly opened at the end of 1908.

Already the Catholics of that country, so wasted and enfeebled by the cold breath of Jansenism and Protestantism, have begun to realize the beneficial results of this sanatorium, where the "Spiritual Cure of St. Ignatius" works such wonders, and have appealed to the sons of Loyola to open a similar house in every diocese of Holland, the bishops, priests and laymen of all ranks of society promising their aid and the funds necessary to found and carry on the work.

About the same time the English Jesuits were endeavouring to follow, on a modest scale, the splendid example of their brethren abroad. In 1908 it was decided to make a trial in the North, where the large Catholic population of Liverpool, Manchester, Preston and other towns had already shown their eagerness for the starting of retreats.

Compstall Hall, a fine house standing in ten acres of ground, near Marple, Cheshire, was rented, and the first retreat given on May 21st, 1908. Representatives from almost every trade were present—carpentry, bricklaying, painting and coopering; hands from the cotton mills, glass-factory, railway-wagon making, a solicitor's clerk, a postmaster, and a local alderman. The result of the attempt to establish Retreats for Workmen in England was awaited with no little interest. The conditions of the countries were very unlike. What appealed to the French or Belgian workman might not suit the temperament of his British comrade. Would the men of the great manufacturing towns of England be able to leave their work for three whole days? Would they be willing to make this sacrifice of time and money? Many thought not, but the triumphant result of the first year's work has more than justified the confidence of the promoters of retreats for these countries.

The figures are as follows:—

	Retreats	Men
May, 1908, to May, 1909	15	270

Consoling as these numbers are they would have been much larger if accommodation could have been provided for all the applicants. As the men were obliged to bear the whole of the expenses themselves, in addition to the loss of half a week's wages, every effort was made to keep the tariff as low as possible, consistent with good catering. By very careful management it was found possible to cover everything by a charge of ten shillings a head for the four days.

The unanimous verdict of all was that it was the holiest and happiest time of their lives—"a treat," as one man said, "and not a retreat."

What Is a Retreat?

The word retreat is well known in these countries, but it does not convey to the mind the full meaning of the French expression, "Retraite Fermée" (enclosed retreat). A short mission, consisting of a series of sermons, without much logical sequence, preached to a mixed congregation of men and women, has come to be known as a retreat. The word is misleading, far removed from the lines laid down by St. Ignatius in his famous book of the Spiritual Exercises. Following the counsel of our Divine Lord to His Apostles, "Come aside and rest awhile," the true exercitant must give up for a while every occupation, even of a charitable nature, and in the quiet and peace of a religious house devote his time to prayer and the interests of his soul. "I will lead her into the wilderness," says Holy Writ, "and there speak to her heart."

"To make a retreat," writes Father Vermeersch, S.J., "is to remove a man far from the noise and dissipation of the world; to tear him from the surroundings in which his life, occupied and distracted as much by pleasure as by worry, is passed; to make him spend three days in solitude face to face with God and himself, occupied only with the grand interests of his soul; to unfold to him the meaning and the end of his present life, humble him before his faults, and having put his conscience in order and peace, propose to him Jesus Christ as a model to imitate, a King whose soldier he is, his Saviour, his God Whom he ought to serve and love. Then combining prayer and silent reflection, the grace of God with personal labour, bring about the complete victory over himself, the transformation of a man into a perfect Christian and an apostle. Thus he will learn to live well, profit by the life God gave him and die a holy death."

A retreat may be summed up as solitude and prayer—a time of repose, yet one of earnest labour. Repose of the weary spirit, repose of heart and conscience; labour of the soul by searching inspection of its inner working; labour by meditation, resolution and prayer.

These days are passed in silence, reflection and exercises of piety. Four times a day all assemble in the chapel, where, in the simplest language, the Director proposes some thoughts on the fundamental truths of religion, the life and Passion of the Redeemer. At the close of the discourse each one retires to his room, and there alone, at the foot of the crucifix or before an image of the Sacred Heart, ponders on what has been said, prays for light and grace, forming the resolutions which are to guide his life afterwards.

In this personal applying to one's own needs the general principles laid down lies the whole secret and success of a retreat.

"It was above all," wrote one man, "when I found myself alone at the foot of my crucifix, turning over in my mind the truths I had just heard, that a profound emotion I cannot describe filled my soul. I am not of an emotional nature, it is true, but it seemed to me as if God *was hammering at my head.*"

God alone knows the miracles of grace wrought in these little cells, or what has passed between Himself and the sinful soul during these moments of prayer.

Sometimes such a note as the following will be left behind:—

"Whoever you are who have come here to meditate in silence and recollection on your last end and the salvation of your soul, remember this: here, at this table, before that crucifix on the wall, a man weighed down with iniquities has been before you, and has wept tears of repentance."

Nothing is neglected to help the soul in this great work of spiritual transformation. Meditations, instructions, reading of pious books, vocal prayer, recitation of the Rosary, visits to the Blessed Sacrament follow one another in quick succession. Each moment of the day has its special duty assigned; nothing is left to the chance inspiration of the moment. A tranquil silence reigns in the house, broken only by the sound of the bell summoning all to the garden, the refectory or chapel.

All too quickly this time, which on the first evening seemed interminable, passes by in prayer and recollection. It has been a new life for those whose days are one long round of toil. Many of them have tasted, for the first time since their youth, the sweets of a peaceful conscience, the joy of friendship with God, and now go out to face the world again with renewed courage and strength, a heart determined to repair the past.

Those who were always faithful to the law of God are animated with new zeal for the building up of Christ's Kingdom, and above all of bringing those around them to make a trial of that retreat, which has worked such wonders in themselves.

Retreat versus Mission

It may be objected against the establishment of retreat houses that the same results can be obtained by the sermons of a public mission. Yet a moment's reflection will show that there is a vast difference between the methods employed and the fruit resulting from a mission and a retreat. The one makes its influence felt only at certain hours in the evening, the other at every hour; the first uses a few well-known means of moving the heart, the other employs every act of the day, all directed towards one definite end; in the mission it is the preacher who does the work, in a retreat the exercitant himself.

Too often the effects of the most successful mission are only temporary. Much good has been done. There has been a revival of faith and energy in well-doing. Many a wandering soul has found its way back to the fold, but with the departure of the missioner, the parish, little by little, returns to its normal condition. The crowds which filled the church nightly are again content with complying with the bare obligations of their religion; the converted sinner or reformed drunkard resume their evil habits, break through their resolutions, and wait for the next mission.

The eloquence of the preacher has indeed stirred souls, but not convinced them.

On the other hand, the efficacy of a retreat consists in personal reflection, favoured by the absence of all distracting occupations and the logical sequence of subjects treated. Solitude, silence and serious reflection, united to fervent prayer, act powerfully upon the soul and cause it to experience sentiments hitherto unknown. The great problems of a present and a future life—sin, its punishments, the service of a God Who is also his Creator—pondered on seriously for the first time appear in a new light. The exercitant finds his soul penetrated by the retreat, and, if aided by the "Means of Perseverance" to be spoken of later, its fruits are, in the vast majority of cases, permanent.

One man wrote down his impressions after his first retreat:— "During the mission my mind was occupied all day with my business; the sermons at night produced an excellent effect, but were soon forgotten in the cares of life. During the retreat the solitude, recollection and suspension of work permitted the soul to enter into herself. The exercises which succeeded one another in order made the great truths penetrate to the bottom of my soul and moved me to generous resolutions."

In the end proposed a mission differs entirely from a retreat. The first has for its objective the great mass of the people, the obstinate sinner rather than the just. Its aim is to convert, to influence the multitude and do a little good to the many.

In striking contrast to this comes the work of a retreat. It appeals not to the indifferent crowd, the careless liver, but to the *élite*, to those who by their intelligence or influence are capable of leading others by their example. It seeks first for the upright and virtuous, the men of character and zeal, and not content with making them better Christians, more solicitous about their own salvation, strives to mould them into lay apostles, thus creating in every parish, writes the Bishop of Tournai, "an *état major* of generous souls determined to bring about the complete reign of our Lord Jesus Christ in souls, in the workshop, in the family."

Lay Apostles

The fruits of a good retreat are many. Peace of mind and joy of heart, the better realization of man's noble destiny, his end in life and the hope of eternal reward awaiting him react powerfully upon his home relations, lessen the burden upon the toiler's shoulders, and brighten an existence often dreary enough. But the greatest and most striking result of the "retraite fermée" is the formation of the lay apostle. During these days of prayerful silence many generous resolutions are formed; foremost among them is the determination "to do" something for God and His interests, to make up for a sinful, wasted life, and bring others to share in the benefits of a retreat.

To lead a virtuous life is something, but this is not enough for him now. He must impart his new-found happiness to others; do good to those about him, raise them up also to more generous things, throw himself into the fight against sin; in a word, become an apostle.

"Since my twenty-five workmen made their retreat, Malines counts twenty-five more apostles," wrote the Dean, asking, at the same time, places for another group. "I cannot tell you how much consolation our exercitants give us. During the recent mission they have been veritable apostles, bringing to the church numbers of their comrades, who, thanks to their example and influence, have trampled on the curse of human respect and have made their peace with God."

At Bruges a series of conferences was poorly attended. An appeal was made to the old exercitants of the town, with the result that each evening the church was filled, and at the close a body of more than 600 men received Communion together.

"I only ask one thing of Almighty God," said a well-known anti-clerical, "that He would allow me to live long enough to rescue from socialism as many souls as I have led into it by my words and evil example."

Another curé in a large manufacturing district writes:— "When I met my men, on their way back from their retreat, I was astounded, they were so happy. They seized me by the hands, thanking me from their hearts, and declaring themselves ready to become the apostles of the parish. They have kept their word, too, for their splendid example preaches more powerfully than my sermons, and they are tireless in making recruits for the coming retreat."

For the average man the opportunities of doing good are necessarily limited. However, in seeking out candidates for a retreat he has always abundant scope for his zeal, and can daily put in practice the motto and aim of the retreats—"The apostolate of workmen by workmen, the ideal to be aimed at." All around him he sees his fellow-workers, some badly in need of a helping hand, others eager to further every work of charity, all possessing untold capabilities for good. To make the retreat known, to bring others under its influence, is the chief work of the lay apostle. To those leading virtuous lives he will first appeal, pointing out the good to be done, urging them to make a practical test of what he advocates. Thus, little by little, a group of the best elements in the district will be formed, all animated with the same spirit and zealous to assist others.

A larger field of action is now open to these earnest workers—the growing mass of the careless and indifferent Catholics, men who have not yet broken with the Church, but whose sole religion consists in a distracted attendance at Sunday Mass and a doubtful Paschal Communion.

Their lives are careless and sinful, but their Faith still strong. The influence of bad companions has dragged them down, evil habits bind them closer and closer in their fatal grip; yet if they could get a fair start again all would be well. A retreat is the remedy, a retreat their only salvation.

The most consoling, if hardest, work yet remains for the lay apostle—the bringing back of those who have wandered from the fold. It would seem as if nothing could move these souls hardened in sin. The words of a devoted priest make no impression; mission after mission leaves them unconverted; the tears and prayers of a wife or daughter remain unanswered, but experience has proved that the word of a comrade, men of their own position, will succeed where every other means has failed. The example of a man, once like himself, who has found at the house of retreat the happiness which sin had driven from his heart appeals to him with irresistible force.

Sometimes the joking taunt of a friend that he is afraid of making the experiment breaks down the barrier of years and brings back the erring one to find in the calm silence of retreat that peace of heart, the joy of a good conscience.

Selection of Candidates for Retreat

As has been pointed out, the intention of the retreat is not directly the conversion of great sinners, nor is its aim merely to cause those who go through it to lead more Christian lives. They are to be the means, in the hands of their priest, of bit by bit making the parish better, the leaven of good which is to spread through the whole mass. Theirs is no longer to be an indifferent, passive Christianity, but an active, living one, full of the tireless zeal of the Apostle, striving "in season and out of season" to promote the glory of God and the good of souls.

Hence it is evident, especially in the beginning, if the retreats are to produce the great results expected from them, that care must be taken in the selection of those who are to make the experiment. Not many, but the BEST, should be chosen, those especially who seem to possess the qualifications for the end in view, or who, either from their position, their popularity, or their exemplary character, are capable of influencing others. Men of every age may be invited, but having regard to the nature of the work for the new apostles and the formation they are to receive, twenty to fifty years would seem to be the limit. Youth is the time of more generous ideas, more eager for works of zeal and more capable of being moulded.

To every church is attached a sodality or confraternity of men. Here the Rev. Director will find gathered the best elements of his parish and the most suitable subjects for a retreat. When once a little group of four or five intelligent men, selected with care, have returned from their first retreat and a beginning made by their example, many others will be found eager to imitate them, who, in turn, will become active propagators of the work. A start is all that is needed, for the best recruiters of a retreat are those who have made one. They are convinced of its practical utility, its beneficial results; there is no reason for suspecting their sincerity, and speaking with conviction their words in turn convince.

In Belgium it has been found that if only one man came from a district he was soon followed by three or four more, and these by larger numbers of their comrades. Many examples might be given:—

The Burgomaster of Laerne sent three men to make a retreat—the first from the town. The following year their number had risen to twenty-eight, and has since gone on steadily increasing. Another gentleman, a sculptor, "was so impressed by the evident good produced that, on his return home, he paid the entire expense of a retreat for twenty-five men living near him.

Preparation for Retreat

As a rule little is gained by a general appeal made to a sodality or large group of men to induce them to make a retreat. The work, to be effective and produce the best results, must be done individually, soul by soul. Ordinarily speaking, men do not suddenly determine to enter on a retreat, and they only go through it with fruit when they have been looking forward to it and preparing for a little while. If the intending exercitants are invited only a few days beforehand, hurried off without sufficient knowledge of the importance of the work before them or what they are going to do, it is only natural that the fruit will be little.

With the view of developing the esteem and desire of this great spiritual benefit and making the work better known, "Preparatory

Leagues for Retreats" have been founded, with great success, especially in Holland and Belgium.

A small committee of three or four zealous men, willing to give their time and energies in furthering the interests of the League, is first formed. At a meeting of the sodalities attached to the church, or during the Sunday Masses, a short explanation of a retreat is given, and pamphlets describing its scope and advantages distributed. The names are then taken of those willing to subscribe a small amount weekly (about 5 cents, or ½d.). The principle is that of the "Propagation of the Faith"—to give little but often, and thus make the thought of retreats enter into the daily life of the people.

In Holland these Leagues have been taken up with wonderful enthusiasm. A few weeks after their foundation the "Retreat League" of Eindhoven numbered over 4,600 members, and even small villages count their subscribers by hundreds.

With the Committee and Spiritual Director of the League rests the choice of candidates for the retreat. They make the necessary arrangements, pay all expenses from the funds collected, and if the contingent is not large enough for a separate retreat, their numbers are supplemented by the committees of other districts. By this system of organization and co-operation, simple yet effective, a large number of men and women are interested in the work, a constant supply of exercitants is kept up, and, in great measure, the difficult question of finance is solved.

Funds

It is evident the work of retreats is a costly one, and this consideration alone would be sufficient to deter the faint-hearted from embarking on the enterprise. For a retreat men and money are required. Of the first there is no lack. "The fields are white for the harvest." Will the second be forthcoming? The example of little Belgium is instructive and encouraging. In the space of little more than fifteen years money has been collected for the erection and furnishing of six magnificent houses of retreat, each costing thousands of pounds. Here, week after week, groups of men, numbering sometimes sixty, spend three whole days going through the "Spiritual Exercises." The cost of each man, including sometimes his railway ticket and a small compensation for the loss of the three days' salary, comes to about fifteen francs. Each year over 10,000 men make a retreat, with such beneficial results that the number of applications is growing steadily. This means that 150,000 francs, or over £6,000, must be found for the yearly maintenance of the work. If to that be added a similar amount for 15,000 women, one can realize the gigantic proportions the "oeuvre des retraites fermées" has assumed in Belgium.

Yet this sum is found, and the cry is not "more men and money," but "more room." How is it done?

The sources of income are numerous. In general, the co-operation of the many rather than the generosity of the few is looked to. Those who are members of a Preparatory League have their expenses covered by the small weekly subscription. On their return from retreat they show even greater energy to collect the means of sending their comrades to share in their new-found joy.

Small committees of ladies and gentlemen, including members of the best families in each town, rival one another in their zeal. A systematic house-to-house collection is made; on every side much generosity and practical sympathy is met, the existence of the retreats becomes better known, and annual subscriptions secured.

Sometimes a wealthy man or generous lady will provide the means necessary for an entire retreat of twenty-five or thirty men, or a priest, anxious to test the effect on his own parish, will sacrifice his well-earned holiday to procure this blessing for his parishioners.

Again, the members of a poor family will unite their scanty savings to send a brother or father, long years away from the Sacraments, to one of these houses of salvation, and invariably the sacrifice wins for him the grace of conversion and brings back to a wretched home peace and joy once more.

Other towns are raising the capital necessary for the "foundation" of retreats, on the same principle that beds are endowed in hospitals or annual Masses established.

The large employers of labour, owners of factories and mines, the heads of leading houses have been quick to see the advantage to themselves and their business accruing from these retreats, and have become their supporters, contributing largely to the expenses. Their motives may not have been disinterested or nothing more than philanthropic, but that which made their men sober, steady, honest and hard-working, content with their lot in life, opposed to the restless, revolutionary spirit of socialism, was certainly deserving of their support. Hence it is no uncommon thing for leading Freemasons and Liberals, bitter enemies of the Church, to send their workmen to make a retreat, paying their expenses and three days' wages as well.

After the Retreat

Those who are skilled in dealing with souls may justly doubt of the marvellous results claimed for the "retraite fermée." They know human nature well; the generosity of which man is capable and his weakness also. Their own experience has taught them how short-lived sometimes are the firmest resolutions, how quickly one loses sight of the high ideals born in an hour of fervour, and how very soon good intentions are abandoned and forgotten. They admit that the immediate results of a retreat are excellent. The men come back deeply impressed with what they have heard and meditated on, full of the best dispositions, eager to impart to others the secret of happiness they have learned, and determined to prove to the world that their lives are not what they once were, But, they think with sorrow, this will not last; the zeal of these new apostles will soon cool and die away; in a very short time the effects of the retreat will have worn off, leaving them little better than they were before.

The organizers of Retreats for Workmen have been the first to admit this objection. They never hoped or expected in three days to root out the evil growth of years, or so completely change a man's character and habits as to make any falling away impossible. They know that heroism is a rare flower indeed; that saints are not cast in moulds and turned out ready-made to order. The retreat has stirred the soil, scattered well the good seed, and removed every obstacle to the action of divine grace upon the soul. Much has been done, but much still remains to do if the harvest is to be great. To send men to a retreat and then leave them entirely to themselves, without any means of sustaining their fervour and recalling their resolutions, is but to plant in a fruitful field and then abandon it. It has been found that defections after retreat are solely due to want of some organization to sustain the good dispositions formed. With this end in view, those who have made a retreat are enrolled in the "League of Retreats." Each month the members meet for Mass and Communion in a body; a short instruction is given to recall to the exercitants their promises and to maintain them in the spirit of fervour.

These Leagues, or "Monthly Recollections," are indispensable for the success of the retreats and perseverance of the men. Their exact form is of little importance provided there is some living organization to bring together and sustain by the force of example those who, if, left to themselves, might grow weary in well-doing. Where a confraternity or association already exists in a parish, admission to its ranks will do much to supply the want of a special League for the exercitants. But it must be borne in mind that such a League has a very definite end. To gather together each month a number of men for prayer, to address a few words of exhortation to them and then peacefully send them to their homes is indeed something, but not enough. The retreat, with its supplementary work—the Monthly Reunion—has a much grander end: the formation of the workingman apostle. It aims at forming round the priest of each church a picked band of laymen always ready to co-operate with him in his work for souls and the glory of God. Full of zeal, desirous of giving a helping hand to their comrades, he will find in these new auxiliaries a powerful lever for good in the parish. On them he can count for the establishing and maintaining any social or charitable scheme for the bettering of his flock; by their means he will reach many a soul who has got beyond his priestly influence, and he will have the consolation of feeling that he is not alone in the awful fight against sin and evil.

The retreat takes in hand these future apostles, moulds them for three days in the school of St. Ignatius and sends them back to their priest full of excellent dispositions. It is for him now to continue the good work by grouping them together, pointing out to them where their energies may be most usefully employed, encouraging, instructing, and guiding them; in short, forming from the material round him fit instruments for the spiritual uplifting of the working classes. If a little care is taken in the selection and preparation of candidates, if, above all, when the retreat is over, they are not abandoned to themselves but given a helping hand and sustained by the monthly meeting of the League, the results of the retreat will be permanent and its fruits consoling above all expectation.

In Belgium, where the organization of workmen's retreats has been brought to a wonderful degree of perfection, this gathering of the men together is looked upon as important as the three days given to the exercises. All over the country these "Retreat Leagues," or "Leagues of Perseverance," are rapidly being established, and already can be numbered by hundreds.

Individually a good-living, fervent Christian is capable of exercising an immense influence on those around him, but here, as elsewhere, "union is strength," and the very example of a united body of men is a powerful factor for good, and an encouragement to them all. The little Flemish village of Alken only counts fifty who have made a retreat, yet their example has been the means of bringing together over 300 men to the monthly Communion.

Some Results and Appreciations

Twenty-five years have passed since the first attempt was made, in the north of France, to get the working classes to make private or "closed" retreats. The test of time has been applied to the work; the result has convinced the sceptic and silenced the scoffer.

Wherever the experiment is made it is found that a retreat is the best and most persuasive school for good. It calms the mind of man; makes of him a staunch Christian, free from human respect, capable of supporting the timid and restraining the licentious; it gives to the home a good father, a faithful and devoted husband, whose example reacts on the family of which he is the head, and thus brings about a religious revival in many houses. "Since my husband made a retreat my house from being a hell has become a paradise. He no longer swears or drinks, and gives me now all his wages."

No sooner is the retreat over than the late exercitants feel the desire growing within them of putting in practice what they have heard, of doing something for God.

"Up to this I have never understood things," an artisan writes; "how true it all is, and I have never thought of it! If I could only fix each word in my head and never forget them. I have learned more in these three days than in all my life."

"Ah, if workingmen only knew these houses of retreats," exclaimed a converted Socialist; "if they only knew that there they would find happiness—true happiness—which the trials and labours of life cannot take from them. I have not always enjoyed this real peace; it was the good God Who, in His infinite mercy, made me find it almost in spite of myself. Would that now I could make an appeal to every one of my fellow-workmen and tell them of this easy means of finding happiness in this life, and the assurance of eternal joy in the next."

His resolutions are not mere paper and ink; he sees there is work to be done, and at once. He persuades first one friend, then another, to imitate his example or come with him to the church.

Thus in some quarters groups of forty men can now be seen going to Mass where a year before none went.

At La Louvière, an industrial centre, Communion for men was practically unknown. Within a year of the first retreat sixty young men had become monthly communicants.

In Hainault and Brabant the number of Communions has risen by hundreds of thousands; in six months the increase of a single parish was more than 900, a result directly due to the good effected by the retreat.

Some have set themselves to stamp out in their workshop or factory the habit of cursing and bad talk. If one of them forgets the compact, he is reminded by: "Comrade, no blasphemy here. Have you not made a retreat?"

Others have thrown themselves heart and soul into the electoral campaign, upon which so many Catholic interests depend, or by their energy have assured the success of religious services, as at Antwerp, where the exercitants of the city gathered 8,000 workmen in the cathedral to celebrate the late Pontifical Jubilee. The good work has found its way into the most hostile quarters; many from being anti-Christian have become ardent champions of the Catholic cause. In Ghent, of the twenty men on the Retreat Committee, half are converted Socialists.

Testimonies, almost without number, to the immense good done and the beneficial results of the Workingmen's Retreats might be quoted. A few must suffice.

The curé of a large Belgian parish writes:—

"Formerly I could not make the few men who consented to hear Mass at the door come into the church. Now every Sunday I see a group of a hundred men, Rosary or prayer book in hand, praying in the middle of the congregation. Before the retreats for workingmen began there were scarcely twenty who made their Easter duty. Now 100 receive Holy Communion each month. All the exercitants are an immense help to me in the various social and charitable works of the parish."

A priest, who calls himself a "convert" to the work of retreats, writes:—

"I am delighted by the result of the Workingmen's Retreat. They returned enchanted with their stay at Xhovémont, and what is better, undoubtedly transformed. I did not believe such a thing possible. I see my mistake now. For the future you will find in me, I can promise you, a devoted auxiliary who will spare no effort to send you the greatest possible number of men. Certainly a priest can do no more salutary work for the men of his parish than to procure them a similar benefit. They come back from the retreat Christians and apostles."

Words of a zealous pastor:—"I cannot thank God enough for the immense good done by the retreats. Our four exercitants have returned enchanted. Next year I hope to send you not four, but forty. With such help it would not take five years to reform the worst parish."

The Dean of M——:—"Your retreats are a blessing for our workmen. All are completely changed. Everyone, young and old, ask me as a favour to be allowed to return later. Up to this, out of two hundred who have made the retreat, only one has been found wanting; all the others are models of constancy and fidelity."

"The 150 men from this district communicate regularly, and are models of fervour. Formerly not one of them had the habit of monthly Communion; now they never allow the First Sunday of the month to pass without approaching the Sacraments....In my daily intercourse with the workmen I see, more and more, how much the retreat has calmed them and put into their hearts a contentment they had never tasted before."

From the Curé at Lierre:—"...Sixty of our men have already made a retreat. Before their departure we who knew their habits and ideas could not help asking ourselves, with a certain fear: 'What will be the result? Will they persevere afterwards?' Thank God, these apprehensions no longer exist. All, without exception, have remained faithful, though many had not entered the church for years. Most of them attend faithfully the various devotions—Benediction, Stations of the Cross, daily Mass. Many have had a good deal to suffer from their change of life—insults, persecution, and even loss of employment.... They are real apostles; they strive to bring back their comrades to a better life; they wage war on bad books and papers, and give a splendid example to their own families. Of their own accord they have established a Sodality of the Sacred Heart, which already counts 450 men. I could mention houses in which formerly one only saw profane pictures or Socialistic emblems where now the crucifix or Mary's statue occupy the place of honour. I could tell of others where prayer was unknown, and now, morning and evening, father, mother and children recite them together. For my part I affirm, without fear of contradiction, that the work of retreats is the most useful work both for the spiritual and temporal good of the toiler, and is a fruitful source of religious regeneration for a parish."

In 1906 the Curé of Mons wrote:—"If I could give a thousand francs a year to help this splendid work, to which I was formerly opposed, I would gladly do so, for it is the work *par excellence*. My parish, when I came to it, had a very bad reputation. Resolved to do the impossible and reform it, I established associations, clubs for the men, etc., but with little apparent effect. Last year, on the advice of a friend, I decided to send forty workmen to the house of retreats. I frankly confess I did not believe in the experiment, but when they returned I was amazed at the result. They seized me by the hands, many of them in tears, They were transformed! I can only repeat, I am a convert. May my example convert many others."

The men are no less eager to testify to the change worked by grace in their souls. A Ghent Socialist says:—

Thanks to the retreat I have become the happiest of men, and nothing will ever separate me again from my God. I was the terror of my wife and children. I led a life of impiety and debauch. But now I feel in heaven, my heart full of joy, peace and contentment, overflowing with a happiness which was unknown to me and which I cannot describe.

The letters of the men are not the least consoling part of the work, and give ample proof of their gratitude to God and the generous benefactors who enabled them to share in the blessings of a retreat:—

"My happiness is now too great to be expressed in words. Thanks, a thousand times thanks, to Almighty God and Mary. O my God, I wish to thank You every day of my life on my knees for the grace of this retreat. I was sunk in despair, but You have saved me on the brink of the abyss."

"If men only knew what a retreat really is, no one would ever refuse to make one. I would give all my fortune for the treasure I have found here."

"It cost me much to come to the retreat, but to leave this house now costs me far more. I have passed three days in heaven."

"Since I made a retreat I no longer know myself, I am so happy."

"I ever think of you," writes a young mechanic to a Jesuit Father, "for I shall never forget the happy hours spent at Xhovémont. Every evening, on my return from work, I turn my eyes to that house of retreats where I have found forgiveness for my sins, and I repeat with joy: 'There it was that the veil, which so long covered my eyes, was torn aside.' O Father! what happiness to see me now completely changed, I who by my words have tried to ruin so many others."

Why Not in Ireland?

Reviewing the wonderful results and the good effected in other countries by Retreats for Workmen, the question naturally suggests itself: "Why not in Ireland?" Are the toilers in our cities and towns less anxious about the salvation of their souls than their comrades of France or Belgium, less capable of leading holy lives and doing a layman's part in the building up of Christ's Kingdom on earth? Or, on the other hand, are our Catholic men so well grounded in their religion, so deeply rooted in their faith, as to have nothing to fear from the prevailing spirit of Materialism and Infidelity?

To the anxious watcher signs are not wanting that we shall not be long secure from the attacks of those who, on the Continent, have worked such havoc in the Church. The voice of the Socialist is heard in the land. The tide of infidel literature, cheap, clever, attractive, is slowly gaining ground, carrying with it the foul poison of doubt and incredulity, sparing nothing, however sacred or holy.

How to save our dear land from such dangers is a problem which must interest every man and woman who has the interests of their country at heart. This was the problem which Catholics in other lands had to face. They saw the efforts made to draw away the toiler from allegiance to his Church, the harm done to home and State by Socialistic doctrines, and the irresistible onward march of modern infidelity. Every effort to stay the progress of the evil was fruitless. Organization was met by organization, Catholic leagues opposed hostile associations with little or no result, till, realizing that the solution of the whole social difficulty was, as Leo XIII pointed out, a question not of parliaments but religion, recourse was had to the now famous "Retreats for Workmen.'"

Their success has astounded the most sceptical. Wherever retreat houses have been opened—in Germany, France, Belgium, Holland, and within the last year in England and Italy—workmen have flocked to them and have gone through the Spiritual Exercises of St. Ignatius with a fervour and earnestness impossible to describe.

If Protestant Holland and England can find hundreds willing to make this sacrifice for their souls and God, if Belgium can yearly send 10,000 men to make a three days' retreat, what might not be done in Catholic Ireland? The faith and generosity of our people would ensure the success of an undertaking, which touches so closely the interests of Jesus, and the influence for good of these workingmen apostles in a parish would soon be apparent.

To those who say: "My men are excellent Catholics, they have no need for a retreat; it would do them no good," we would answer: "Try its effects and you will see." As a venerable priest remarked: "Each pastor thinks his own flock the best in the world, and I did the same, but now that my men have made their retreat I see there is still much to be done."

In conclusion, the words of our present saintly Pontiff should stimulate our zeal and generosity: "One cannot conceive a better method for saving the workingmen exposed, at the present time, to so many dangers. Since Our elevation to the Papal Throne We see still more the importance of these retreats for the end We have in view, 'To restore all things in Christ.'"

"We desire," wrote Leo XIII, "to see this work, so happily commenced in France and Belgium, spread with equal success among other nations."

To strive and give effect in Ireland to this wish of the dead Pontiff, by making the nature and scope of Workingmen's Retreats better known, is the object of this pamphlet.

Vocations

Nihil obstat: Joannes Keane, S.J., *Cens. Theol. Dep.*

Imprimi potest: Eduardus, *Archiep. Dublinen.,*
Dublini, Jan., 1928, Hiberniae Primas.

"Blessed are they that dwell in Thy house, O Lord, they shall praise Thee for ever and ever."

—Ps. 35

"Alas, alas, for those who die without fulfilling their mission! who were called to be holy, and lived in sin; who were called to worship Christ, and who plunged into this giddy and unbelieving world; who were called to fight, and remained idle. Alas for those who have had gifts and talents, and have not used, or misused, or abused them! The world goes on from age to age, but the holy Angels and blessed Saints are always crying, alas, alas, and woe, woe, over the LOSS OF VOCATIONS, and the disappointment of hopes, and the scorn of God"s love, and the ruin of souls."

—Newman

"Come, Follow Me"

"Good Master, what good shall I do that I may have life everlasting?" It was the eager question of one whom fortune had blessed with the wealth of this world, but who realised that life eternal was a far more precious treasure. He had come to the Divine Teacher, seeking what he must yet do to make secure the great prize for which he was striving. He was young and wealthy, a ruler in the land, one whose life had been without stain or blemish.

"The Commandments?—All these have I kept from my youth," he had said; "Good Master, what is yet wanting to me?" Jesus looked on him with love, for such a soul was dear to His Sacred Heart. "If thou wilt be perfect," comes the answer, "go sell what thou hast and give to the poor, and come, follow Me."

There was a painful pause: nature and grace were struggling for the mastery; the invitation had been given, the road to perfection pointed out. There was only one sacrifice needed to make him a true disciple, but it was a big one, too great for him who lately seemed so generous. He hesitates, wavers, and then sadly turns away, with the words "Come, follow Me," ringing in his ears, for love of his great possessions had wrapt itself round his heart—a Vocation had been offered and refused. "What a cloud of misgivings," says Father Faber, "must hang over the memory of him whom Jesus invited to follow Him. Is he looking now in heaven upon that Face from whose mild beauty he so sadly turned away on earth?"

Nearly two thousand years have passed since then, but unceasingly that same Voice has been whispering in the ears of many a lad and maiden, "One thing is yet wanting to you—come, follow Me." Some have heard that voice with joy and gladness of heart, and have risen up at the Master's call; others have stopped their ears, or turned away in fear from the side of Him Who beckoned to them, while not a few have stood and listened, wondering what it meant, asking themselves could such an invitation be for them, till Jesus of Nazareth passed by and they were left behind for ever.

To these, chiefly, is this simple explanation of a Vocation offered, in the hope that they may recognise the workings of grace within their souls, or be moved to beg that they may one day be sharers in this crowning gift of God's eternal love.

What Is a Vocation?

"How do I know whether I have a vocation or not?" How often this question has risen to the lips of many a young boy or girl, who has come to realise that life has a purpose, only to be brushed aside with an uneasy "I am sure I have not," or a secret prayer that they might be saved from such a fate! How little they know the happiness they are throwing away in turning from God's invitation, for such a question, and such a feeling, is often the sign of a genuine vocation.

In the first place, a vocation, or "a call to the Priesthood or the Religious Life," in contradistinction to the general invitation, held out to all men, to a life of perfection, even in the world, is a free gift of God bestowed on those whom He selects: "You have not chosen Me," he said to His Disciples, "but I have chosen you," and the Evangelist tells us that "Christ called unto Him whom He willed." Often that invitation is extended to those whom we would least expect. Magdalen, steeped to the lips in iniquity, became the spouse of the Immaculate; Matthew, surrounded by his ill-gotten gains; Saul, "breathing out threatenings and slaughter against the Christians," each heard that summons, for a sinful life in the past, St. Thomas teaches, is no impediment to a vocation.

But though this gift is of surpassing value and a mark of very special affection on His part, God will not force its acceptance on the soul, leaving it free to correspond with the grace or reject it. Some day the Divine Hunter draws near the prey which He has marked out for the shafts of His love; timidly, as if fearing to force the free will, He whispers a word. If the soul turns away, Jesus often withdraws forever, for He only wants willing volunteers in His service. But if the startled soul listens, even though dreading lest that Voice speak again, and shrinking from what It seems to lead her to, grace is free to do its work and bring her captive to the Hunter's feet.

Unconsciously, in that first encounter, she has been deeply wounded with a longing for some unknown, as yet untasted, happiness. Almost imperceptibly a craving for a nobler life has taken possession of the heart; prayer and self-denial, the thought of sacrifice, bring a new sweetness; the blazing light of earthly pleasures, once so dazzling, seems to die away; the joys, the amusements, of the world no longer attract or satisfy; their emptiness serves only to weary and disgust the more, while through it all the thirst for that undefinable "something" tortures the soul.

"Sweet and tender Lord!" exclaims the Blessed Henry Suso, "from the days of my childhood my mind has sought for something with burning thirst, but what it is I have not as yet fully understood. Lord, I have pursued it many a year, but I never could grasp it, for I know not what it is, and yet it is something that attracts my heart and soul, without which I can never attain true rest. Lord, I sought it in the first days of my childhood in creatures, but the more I sought it in them the less I found it, for every image that presented itself to my sight, before I wholly tried it, or gave myself quietly to it, warned me away thus: "I am not what thou seekest." Now my heart rages after it, for my heart would so gladly possess it. Alas! I have so constantly to experience what it is not! But what it is, Lord, I am not as yet clear. Tell me, beloved Lord, what it is indeed, and what is its nature, that secretly agitates me."

Even in the midst of worldly pleasure and excitement there is an aching void in the heart. "How useless it all is!—how hollow!—how unsatisfying! Is this what my life is to be always? Was I made only for this?"

Slowly one comes to understand the excellence and advantage of evangelical perfection, the indescribable charm of virginity, and the nobleness of a life devoted wholly to the service of God and the salvation of souls. Louder and stronger has grown the faint whisper, "Come, follow Me," till at last, with an intense feeling of joy and gratitude, or even, at times, a natural repugnance and fear of its responsibilities, the weary soul realises that "The Master is here and calls for thee"—that she has got a Vocation.

A True Vocation

A vocation, therefore, speaking generally, is not the mysterious thing some people imagine it to be, but simply the choice God makes of one for a certain kind of life. "A person is known to have a true vocation to enter a particular career in life," writes Father C. Coppens, S.J., "if he feels sincerely convinced, as far as he can judge with God's grace, that such a career is the best for him to attain the end for which God places him on earth, and is found fit by his talents, habits and circumstances, to enter on that career with a fair prospect of succeeding in the same."

Père Poulain, S.J., the great French ascetical writer, adds: "In order to judge whether we have a vocation that is inspired by

God, it is not usually sufficient to satisfy ourselves that we have a persistent attraction for it. This mark is not certain unless a natural condition is fulfilled, namely, that we have certain physical, moral and intellectual qualities also."

A vocation to the religious state supposes, then, not only a supernatural inclination or desire to embrace it, but an aptitude or fitness for its duties. God cannot act inconsistently. If He really wishes one to follow Him, He must give him the means of doing so, and hence if real obstacles stand in the way, e.g., serious infirmities, an old parent to support, etc., such a one is not called to enter religion.

God at times inspires a person to do something which He does not really wish or intend to be carried out. Thus David longed to build the Temple of the Lord; Abraham was told to sacrifice his son, merely to test their obedience and willingness; for, says St. Teresa, "God is sometimes more pleased with the desire to do a thing than with its actual accomplishment."

St. Francis de Sales regards "a firm and decided will to serve God" as the best and most certain sign of a true vocation, for the Divine Teacher had once said, "If you *wish*…come, follow Me." He writes: "A genuine vocation is simply a firm and constant will desirous of serving God, in the manner and in the place to which He calls me…I do not say this wish should be exempt from all repugnance, difficulty or distaste. Hence a vocation must not be considered false because he who feels himself called to the religious state no longer experiences the same sensible feeling which he had at first, and that he even feels a repugnance and such a coldness that he thinks all is lost. It is enough that his *will* persevere in the resolution of not abandoning its first design.

"In order to know whether God wills one to be a religious, there is no need to wait till He Himself speaks to us, or until He sends an angel from Heaven to signify His will; nor is there any need to have revelations on the subject, but the first movement of the inspiration must be responded to, and then one need not be troubled if disgust or coldness supervene."

Signs of a Vocation

The following is a list of some of the ordinary indications of a vocation, taken principally from the works of Father Gautrelet, S.J., and the *Retreat Manual*. No one need expect to have all these marks, but if some of them are not perceived, the person may safely say he has no vocation:

1. A desire to have a religious vocation, together with the conviction that God is calling you. This desire is generally most strongly felt when the soul is calm, after Holy Communion, and in time of retreat.

2. A growing attraction for prayer and holy things in general, together with a longing for a hidden life and a desire to be more closely united to God.

3. To have a hatred of the world, a conviction of its hollowness and insufficiency to satisfy the soul. This feeling is generally strongest in the midst of worldly amusement.

4. A fear of sin, into which it is so easy to fall, and a longing to escape from the dangers and temptations of the world.

5. It is sometimes the sign of a vocation when a person fears that God may call them; when he prays not

to have it and cannot banish the thought from his mind. If the vocation is sound, it will soon give place to an attraction, though Father Lehmkuhl says: "One need not have a natural inclination for the religious life; on the contrary, a divine vocation is compatible with a natural repugnance for that state."

6. To have zeal for souls. To realise something of the value of an immortal soul, and to desire to co-operate in their salvation.

7. To desire to devote our whole life to obtain the conversion of one dear to us.

8. To desire to atone for our own sins or those of others, and to fly from the temptations which we feel too weak to resist.

9. An attraction for the state of virginity.

10. The happiness which the thought of religious life brings, its spiritual helps, its peace, merit and reward.

11. A longing to sacrifice oneself and abandon all for the love of Jesus Christ, and to suffer for His sake.

12. A willingness in one not having any dowry, or much education, to be received in any capacity, is a proof of a real vocation.

Motives for Entering Religion

St. Francis de Sales writes as follows: "Many enter religion without knowing why they do so. They come into a convent parlour, they see nuns with calm faces, full of cheerfulness, modesty and content, and they say to themselves: 'What a happy place this is! Let us come to it. The world frowns on us; we do not get what we want there.'

"Others come in order to find peace, consolation and all sorts of sweetness, saying in their minds: 'How happy religious are! They have got safe away from all their home worries; from their parents' continual ordering about and fault-finding—let us enter religion.'

"These reasons are worth nothing. Let us consider whether we have sufficient courage and resolution to crucify and annihilate ourselves, or rather to permit God to do so. You must understand what it is to be a religious. It is to be bound to God by the continual mortification of ourselves, and to live only for Him. Our heart is surrendered always and wholly to His Divine Majesty; our eyes, tongue, hands and all our members serve Him continually. Look well into your heart and see if you have resolution enough to die to yourself and to live only to God. Religion is nothing else than a school of renunciation and self-mortification."

As the call to religious life is supernatural, a vocation springing solely from a purely human motive—such as those spoken of by St. Francis—the desire of pleasing one's parents, or some temporal advantage, would not be the work of grace. However, if the *principal* motive which inclines us to embrace the religious state is supernatural, the vocation is a true one, for Divine Providence often makes use of the trials and misfortunes of life to fill a soul with disgust for the world and prepare it for a greater grace.

St. Romuald, founder of the Camaldolese, to escape the consequences of a duel in which he had taken part, sought an asylum in a monastery, where he was so struck by the happy lives of the monks that he consecrated himself to God.

St. Paul, the first hermit, fled to the desert to avoid persecution, and found in the solitude a peace and joy he had long sought in vain. How many eyes have been rudely opened to the shortness and uncertainty of life by the sudden death of a dear friend, and made to realise that the gaining of life eternal was "the one thing necessary"; thwarted ambition, the failure of cherished hopes or the disappointment of a loving heart, have convinced many a future saint that the only Master worth serving is Jesus Christ, His affection the only love worth striving for.

Hence we may conclude with the learned theologian, Lessius, "If anyone takes the determination of entering religion, well resolved to observe its laws and duties, there is no doubt that this resolution, this vocation, comes from God, whatever the circumstances which seem to have produced it."

"It matters little how we commence, provided we are determined to persevere and end well," says St. Francis de Sales; and St. Thomas lays it down that "no matter from what source our resolution comes of entering religion, it is from God"; while Suarez maintains that "generally the desire for religious life is from the Holy Ghost, and we ought to receive it as such."

Should We Encourage Vocations?

It is a curious fact that although many pious and learned persons do not shrink from discouraging, in every possible way, aspirants to religious life, they would scruple to give them any help or encouragement. "A vocation must be entirely the work of the Holy Ghost," they say. Willingly they paint the imaginary difficulties and trials of a convent life, and hint at the unhappiness sometimes to be found there; they speak of the long and serious deliberation necessary before one takes such a step, and thus, unintentionally perhaps, but most effectually, extinguish the glowing enthusiasm of a youthful heart.

Some even assume a terrible responsibility by deliberately turning away souls from the way into which the Master is calling them, forgetting the warning: "It is I who have chosen you," never reflecting on the irretrievable harm they are causing by spoiling the work of God.

Others calmly assure a postulant, who has been found unsuitable for a particular Order, that this is a certain sign Almighty God does not want him, that he has no vocation and should not try again.

It is quite true to say that a vocation comes from above, but God's designs can be hindered or helped by His creatures, and He has ever made use of secondary agents in their execution. The formation of character and the direction of the steps of the young towards the Sanctuary is largely in the hands of parents and teachers; how many a happy priest and nun daily thank their Maker for the gift of a good mother, who first sowed the seeds of a vocation in their childish heart.[1] Fathers and mothers constantly put before their children the various callings and professions of life to help them in their choice; is the grandest life of all, the service of the King of Kings, the battling for precious

---

[1] Mrs. Vaughan, mother of the Cardinal, spent an hour each evening, for twenty years, praying that all her children might be religious. Her five daughters entered convents, and six out of the eight sons became priests; the remaining two entered a seminary, but found they were not suited for the life.—*Life of Cardinal Vaughan*

souls, and the extension of Christ's Kingdom, to be ignored and never spoken of?

The saints realised that God looked to them to aid Him in the work of fostering vocations. St. Jerome writes thus to Heliodorus: "I invite you, make haste. You have made light of my entreaties; perhaps you will listen to my reproaches. Effeminate soldier! What are you doing under the paternal roof? Hasten to enlist under the banner of Christ."

So eloquently did St. Bernard speak of the advantages of the religious life that all his brothers and thirty young nobles followed him to the solitude of Citeaux.

More striking still was the bringing of the Apostles to Our Lord by indirect means. St. Andrew and St. John were sent to the Saviour by St. John the Baptist: "Behold the Lamb of God. And the two disciples heard him speak, and they followed Jesus."

"Andrew *findeth* first his brother Simon,…and he *brought* him to Jesus."

"On the following day he [Andrew] would go forth into Galilee, and he *findeth* Philip…Philip *findeth* Nathaniel, and said to him: We have found Him of Whom the prophets did write… and Nathaniel said to him: Can any good come out of Nazareth? Philip said to him: Come and see," with the result that he also received the call to follow Christ.

Thus one by one the Apostles were brought to the knowledge of the Messiah and under the influence of His grace, without which all human efforts are useless to produce a vocation. "Know well," says St. Thomas, "that whether it be the suggestion of the devil or the advice of a man which inclined us to the religious life, and makes us thus walk in the footsteps of Jesus Christ, this suggestion or advice is powerless and inefficient so long as God does not attract us inwardly towards Him. Therefore, the proposal of entering into religion, in whatever way it may be suggested to us, can come only from God."

"No man can come to Me, unless it be given him by My Father." Hence the Saint adds, that even if the religious vocation came from the devil, it ought to be embraced as an excellent counsel given by an enemy.

Trying a Vocation

Spiritual writers tell us the evil spirit strives in every possible way to hinder all the good he can. If he cannot turn one away completely from the determination of giving oneself to God, he will work, might and main, to defer the moment as long as possible, knowing that a person in the world is constantly exposed to the danger of losing both the grace of God and "the pearl of great price," his vocation. He knows that until the doors of the monastery have closed behind the young Levite he has every chance of snatching away that treasure. He will lay traps and pitfalls, stir up doubts and fears; he will make the attractions of a life of pleasure seem almost irresistible, causing the bravest heart to waver; "I never realised how dear the world was to me until I had to leave it" has been the agonising cry of many.

Under one pretext or another he induces them to put off their generous resolution from day to day. "O Lord," exclaims St. Augustine, "I said I will come presently; wait a moment; but this presently never came, and this moment did not end. I always resolved to give myself to You on the morrow, and never immediately."

How fatal this delay in responding to the call of God has been those can best tell whom age or altered circumstances have hindered from carrying out their first intention.

If the vocation is *doubtful*, there is need of deliberation, and it must be serious, for hastiness and want of reflection would be unpardonable in such a matter; but so enormous are the advantages to be reaped from a life devoted to God's service, it would be a far greater calamity to miss a vocation through excessive prudence than to mistake a passing thought for the Master's call.

It is well to remember that a person who felt he had no vocation would not sin by embracing the religious state, provided he had the intention of fulfilling all its obligations and serving God to the best of his ability. For, in the opinion of the Angelic Doctor, God will not refuse the special graces, necessary for such a life, to one who sincerely desires to promote His glory.

Our Lord tells us to learn a lesson from "the children of this world, who are wiser in their generation"; there is no hesitation about accepting a tempting offer of marriage, which binds one perhaps to an unsuitable partner, for life; it is worldly wisdom not to delay about such a step when there is a chance of being well settled; and yet St. Ignatius teaches that there is more need for deliberation about remaining in the world than for leaving it. He says: "If a person thinks of embracing a secular life, he should ask and desire more evident signs that God calls him to a secular life than if there were question of embracing the Evangelical Counsels. Our Lord Himself has exhorted us to embrace His Counsels, and, on the other hand, He has laid before us the great dangers of a secular life; so that, if we rightly conclude, revelations and extraordinary tokens of His will are more necessary for a man entering upon a life in the world than for one entering the religious state."

Endless harm has been done by well-meaning people, who, under pretext of "trying a vocation," keep their children from entering a religious house for years.

They urge that getting "to know the world" will develop their faculties and enable them to understand their own mind better; that such a process will broaden their views and help them to judge things at their proper value; finally, that a vocation which cannot stand such a trial, the buffeting of dangerous temptations, and the seductive allurements of worldly pleasure, to which it has been unnecessarily exposed, is no vocation and had far better be abandoned.

"Is the world the place for testing a vocation?" asks St. Vincent de Paul. "Let the soul hasten as fast as possible to a secure asylum." The Church, realising well the necessity of such a trial, prescribes at least a year of probation in every novitiate before admitting candidates to the religious profession. There, safe from the contagious atmosphere of a corrupt world, with abundant time for prayer and thought, with liberty to remain or leave at will, each one can test for himself the sincerity of the desire he felt to abandon all things and follow Christ, before he binds himself irrevocably by his vows.

"One could not give a more pernicious counsel than this" writes Father Lessius. "What is it in reality except to desire to extinguish the interior spirit, under the pretext of a trial, and to expose to the tempests of temptation him who was preparing to gain the port of safety?

"If a gardener were to plant a precious seed, requiring great care, in stony ground, covered with thorns; if he exposed it to the rays of the sun and every change of climate to try whether it would it grow in that unfavourable spot, who would not look upon him as a fool? Those who advise people called to religious life to remain, for a while, in the world have even less sense. A vocation is a divine inspiration; it is a seed fallen upon the earth to bear fruit for eternal life. It is planted in the human heart, a soil little suited to its nature, and requires great care and attention. Watch must be kept that the birds of the air, the demons, do not carry it away; that thorns, the concupiscences and solicitudes of the world, do not choke it; that men with their false maxims should not trample it under foot. Whosoever wishes to preserve and see grow in his heart the seed which the Divine Sower has cast there, ought to fly from the world and reach a safe refuge as soon as possible."

Deliberation

It follows from what has been said that once the voice of God is recognised, that is, when the thought of leaving the world has been more or less constantly before the mind for some time, and the soul realises, even though she dreads it, that "the Lord hath need of her," the call ought to be obeyed promptly.

St. Thomas holds that the invitation to a more perfect life ought to be followed without delay, for these lights and inspirations from God are transient, not permanent, and therefore the divine call should be obeyed instantly. As of old, when He worked His miracles and went about doing good, "Jesus of Nazareth passeth by"; if we do not take advantage of His passing, He may never return. "I stand at the door and knock," He said. "If any man shall hear My voice and open to Me, I will come in to him," if not, that call may never come again.

"Make haste, I beseech you," exclaims St. Jerome, "and rather cut than loosen the rope by which your bark is bound fast to the land," for even a day's delay deprives a person of invaluable merit, which he would acquire in religion.

Delay is dangerous, and long deliberation, as Mgr. Malou assures us, is unnecessary: "Of all the states of life the religious state is, without contradiction, that which demands the least deliberation, and is that of which the choice should cause less doubt, and provoke the least hesitation; for it is in this state that fewer difficulties are met with, and the best means are found for saving our souls."

Age for Entering

"It is well for a man to have borne the yoke from his youth," says Holy Scripture. Mindful of this counsel, and realising that the pure heart of the young receive the impressions of virtue without difficulty, and easily form good habits, that it is above all the time of earnestness and generosity, the Church has always encouraged her children to give themselves to her service from their tender years. The Council of Toledo laid it down: "As soon as a child has arrived at adolescence, that is to say, at the age of twelve for girls and fourteen for boys, they may freely dispose of themselves by entering religion." It is not forbidden to enter at any age; the Council of Trent simply ordained that no one should be admitted to profession before the age of sixteen years complete, but it did not forbid entrance before that time.[2]

---

[2] According to recent legislation of the Holy See, novices are not to be revived below the age of fifteen. Experience has proved that a much larger

Special provision was made in the Rule of St. Benedict for the admission of little children, who were offered by their parents to be educated and thereafter perpetually to persevere in the Order.

"The reception of a child in those days was almost as solemn as a profession in our own. His parents carried him to the church. Whilst they wrapped his hand, which held the petition, in the sacred linen of the altar, they promised, in the presence of God and of His Saints, stability in his behalf. Little beings of three or four years old were brought in the arms of those who gave them life, to accept at their bidding the course in which that life was to run. They were brought into the sanctuary, received the cowl, and took their places as monks in the monastic community."

St. Benedict was only twelve when he entered the cloister, and St. Thomas of Aquin barely fourteen. St. Catherine of Ricci was professed at thirteen; Blessed Imelda died in a Dominican Convent at the age of eleven, and St. Rose of Lima had vowed her chastity to God while only five. In our own days Soeur Thérêse, "The Little Flower," was scarcely fifteen when she entered the Carmelite monastery at Lisieux.

"The Spirit breatheth where He will." There is no rule for vocations, no age-limit for the Call. Innocence attracts the gaze of God, deep-rooted habits of sin, provided they are not persevered in, do not always repel Him. One comes because the world disgusts him, another loves it and leaves it with regret; docility draws down more graces, while resistance often increases the force

percentage of subjects persevere among those who enter between the ages of sixteen and twenty than among those who enter when they are older.

of His invitation. The little child hears His whisperings, while others have not been summoned till years were far advanced.

So jealous is the Church of this liberty for her children that the Council of Trent excommunicates those who, by force or fear, hinder anyone from entering religion without just cause.

As parents often exceed the authority given them by God over their children, in the question of a choice of life, it will be well here to quote the words of the great Jesuit Moralist, Father Ballerini:—"Paternal power cannot take away the right which sons and daughters have to make their own choice of a state of life, and, if they will, to follow Christ's Counsels. The duty, however, which filial piety demands ought not to be disregarded, and the leave of parents ought to be asked. If it is refused, their children ought not at once to take their departure, but should wait for some little time till the parents have realised their obligations. If, however, there should be danger of the parents unjustly hindering the fulfilment of their children's vocation, they may and ought to go without their parents' knowledge. Parents have a right to make some trial of the vocation of their children before they enter; it is not, however, lawful for them to insist that they should first taste the pleasures of the world. If they should happen to be affected by these, the parents would not have reason to conclude that there had not been a true vocation. There may be a true vocation which has been wrongfully abandoned."

St. Liguori quotes a number of theologians who hold that "Parents who prevent their children from entering religion *sin mortally*." "To turn one from a religious vocation," says St. Jerome, "is nothing else than to slay Jesus Christ in the heart of another."

Importance of Following a Vocation

There is no more important moment in the life of a young boy or girl than when "they stand with trembling feet" at the parting of the ways. With St. Paul they had said: "When I was a child, I spoke as a child, I thought as a child," but the days of irresponsible childhood are gone for ever, and now they must launch their bark alone on the stormy waters of life and steer their course for eternity. It is a solemn moment, a time big with possibilities for good or evil, for the youth is face to face with the question what he must do with his future life, a choice upon which not merely his happiness on earth, but even his eternal salvation, may depend.

He has been made by his Creator and given a precious gift to spend it in a certain, definite way, marked out from all eternity by the hand of Divine Providence. What that life is to be for many circumstances and surroundings clearly indicate. But in the hearts of others arises a violent storm from the clashing of rival interests. On the one hand comes the call of the world, the pleading of human nature for a life of ease and pleasure; on the other, the Voice of Christ, softly yet clearly, "Come, follow ME—I have need of you—I have work for you to do."

This, then, is the meaning of his life, the reason why he was drawn out of nothingness, "to Work the works of Him Who sent Him." Is he free to hesitate? Is it a matter of indifference for him to live in a God-chosen state of life or in a self-chosen one, now that his vocation is certain?

To this question St. Liguori answers: "Not to follow our vocation, when we feel called to the religious state, is not a mortal sin; the Counsels of Christ, from their nature, do not oblige under this penalty. However, in regard to the dangers to which our salvation is exposed, in choosing a state of life against the Divine Will, such conduct is rarely free from sin, much more so when a person is persuaded that in the world he places himself in danger of losing his soul by refusing to follow his vocation."

Though one would not sin mortally by refusing to follow a clear Vocation, since it is an invitation, not a command, a person would certainly run a great risk of imperilling his salvation by so acting. God foresees the temptations and dangers of each one; some He knows would never save their souls in the midst of a sinful world, and these He calls away to protect them from its dangers. To the vocation He has attached helps and graces to strengthen the weak soul, but deprived of this help—for God may refuse to give them in the world the graces He would have granted in religion—many will find salvation extremely difficult.

Hence, though the deliberate refusal to correspond to the Divine vocation does not necessarily imply the commission of sin, even when the call is clear and unmistakable, yet it is a serious responsibility, without sufficient reason, to refuse to correspond to such an invitation, offered with so much love and liberality; for a vocation not only shows God's eagerness for the sanctification of the person called to follow in His footsteps, but implies that the Saviour looks for his constant cooperation in "the divinest of all works," the salvation of human souls.[3]

---

[3] "I think it is no exaggeration to say that every priest is the means of saving at least five thousand souls from being lost eternally in Hell."—Archbishop Lynch of Toronto

Can it be wondered at, then, that, deprived of the special graces destined for them, the lives of those who have refused to follow, or have abandoned, a decided vocation are generally unhappy, and, too often, as every confessor knows, sullied with great and numerous sins?

Opposition

Seeing the immense importance of a vocation, and how much depends upon it, both for ourselves and others, it is only natural to expect that the evil one should stir up a regular hornet's nest of opposition. He will prevent it if he can and will not give up the fight without a fierce struggle. Checked and defeated in one direction, he renews his attacks, with greater audacity, in another, striving by delays, disappointments and interior trials to weary the soul and turn it in the end from its resolve. It has been truly said that we never fully realise the number of enemies we have to contend with until the moment we make up our mind resolutely to serve God; one certainly never knew how many people were so keenly interested in our future happiness, so anxious to warn us of the difficulties and dangers of our proposed step, until it became known we were entering religion.

When a young man resolves to renounce the world, his so-called friends rally round him, begging of him not to be such a coward as to run away from what clearly is his duty. They remind him of all the good he might do by staying where he is, but his conscience assures him there is nothing better he can do than go where God, his Master, bids him. They ask him is he a mad fool to give up all the amusements and pleasures he might lawfully enjoy; would it not be better for him first "to see life," before he buries himself in a gloomy cloister; they taunt him with want of moral courage and call him hard-hearted and cruel to desert a loving father or mother in their declining years.

What a terrific struggle it all is he only knows who has been through it. To be told one is simply selfish when one wants only to be generous; to meet with nothing but coldness, cynicism and discouragement when most of all there is an agonising cry in the soul for kindness and sympathy, is hard indeed for flesh and blood to bear, even for the love of Jesus. God, too, Who at first "had disposed all things sweetly" to wean the soul from earthly love and draw it to Himself, in the end sometimes seems to hide His face and abandon His spouse. "It seemed to me," the holy Mother Kerr used to say, "that all my wish for religious life vanished from the moment I decided to follow it."

Doubts and fears give place to the joy and yearning for a life of sacrifice, which formerly filled the heart. St. Teresa, however, tells us not to fear, for this trial, if bravely borne, will lead to greater happiness.

"When an act is done for God alone," she writes, "it is His will before we begin it that the soul, in order to increase its merit, should be afraid; and the greater the fear, if we do but succeed, the greater the reward and the sweetness thence afterwards resulting. I know this from experience; and so, if I had to advise anybody, I would never counsel anyone, to whom good inspirations may come, to resist them through fear of the difficulty of carrying them into effect; there is no reason of being afraid of failure since God is omnipotent.

"Though I could not at first bend my will to be a nun, I saw that the religious state was the best and safest. And thus, by little and little, I resolved to force myself into it. The struggle lasted three months. I used to press this reason against myself: The trials and sufferings of living as a nun cannot be greater than those of Purgatory, and I have well deserved to be in Hell. It is not much to spend the rest of my life as if I were in Purgatory, and then go straight to Heaven. The devil put before me that I could not endure the trials of religious life, because of my delicate nature. I was subject to fainting-fits, attended with fever, for my health was always weak. I defended myself against him by alleging the trials which Christ endured, and that it was not too much for me to suffer something for His sake; besides, He would help me to bear it. I remember perfectly well that the pain I felt when I left my father's house was so great (he would never give his consent to my entering) that I do not believe the pain of dying will be greater, for it seemed to me as if every bone in my body were wrenched asunder. When I took the habit, Our Lord at once made me understand how He helps those who do violence to themselves, in order to serve Him. I was filled with a joy so great that it has never failed me to this day."

Objections

To make matters worse, we play into the hands of the Tempter by listening to his objections, or building up for ourselves imaginary difficulties, which may never occur, forgetting that with the call comes the special "Grace of Vocation," with which, as the Apostle assures us, "we can do all things."

1. "*I may not persevere.*"—Were one to hesitate before a possible failure, little would be done in the world, but the Church wisely

guards against this danger by giving the aspirant to Religion ample time, in the noviceship, to try if he is really called or suited for such a life. To leave or be dismissed from the house of probation is no disgrace, but simply shows God has other designs on the soul. St. Joseph of Cupertino was several times refused admission into the Franciscan Order as unsuitable. He entered the Capuchins, but was sent away, after eight months' trial, because it was thought he had no vocation. Out of compassion he was then received by the Franciscans, with whom he lived till his saintly death.

Suarez tells us we are to consider less our own strength in the matter than the help of grace, for it is in God we must particularly trust. He will not desert us if only we are faithful to His inspirations. If He calls those who do not seek Him, much more will He aid and protect those who have obeyed His call.

"If I did but know that I should persevere," says the author of the Imitation, "and presently he heard within himself an answer from God: 'Do now what thou wouldst do then, and thou shalt be very secure.'"

Instead of being frightened at the sight of a few who have been inconstant in their vocation, St. John Chrysostom says, why not consider the great number of those who, faithful to their engagements, find in Religion peace, happiness and salvation?

2. *"My health may break down."* —No religious is ever dismissed, after Profession, through ill-health. Should God not give sufficient strength for the duties of the novitiate, it is an evident sign that He wants the novice elsewhere. Thus St. Benedict Joseph Labre, finding himself unable to persevere with either the Cistercians or Carthusians, and having tried in vain, for two years, to

enter among the Trappists, saw that his vocation lay in another direction, the perfect imitation, in the world, of the humble, suffering life of his Master. Experience has proved in numberless cases that the regular Community life is of immense benefit to those of feeble health, and God rewards the generous spirit and trust of one willing to serve Him in the midst of infirmities, by giving new vigour and strength.

Père Surin, S.J., advised his mother to become a Carmelite nun at the age of fifty-six. So delicate had she been that she required the constant attendance of four nurses, yet during the fifteen years she lived in the convent, observing all the austerities of the Rule, she never once entered the infirmary.

Another Carmelite, Madame Soyecourt, who died at the age of eighty, had never even abstained in the world on account of ill-health.

St. Bernard served God faithfully for sixty-three years, never relaxing his penances, fasting or labours, though from his entry into religion he was extremely delicate and constantly spat blood.

3. *"I should break my parents' heart."*—When the devil sees in anyone a religious vocation, he does everything possible to prevent him following that attraction. But of all the means he makes use of, the love of one's parents is the most powerful and dangerous. He shows it to be so just and reasonable, he makes use of such specious sophisms, that the poor soul does not know to which voice to listen—that which calls him or that which bids him go back.

St. Alphonsus Liguori declared that the hardest trial of all his life was when he made known to his father his determination of quitting the world. "Dear father, I see that you suffer for my sake. However, I must declare that I no longer belong to this world: God has called me, and I am determined to follow His voice." For three hours the father clasped him in his arms weeping and repeating, "My son, do not leave me! Oh, my son, my son! I do not deserve this treatment." If he had listened to this pathetic appeal the Church would have lost one of her grandest saints; fortunately he remembered the words of Him Who could call Himself "the kindest and gentlest of men": "Do not think that I came to send peace upon earth: I came not to send peace but the sword. For I came to separate the son from the father, and the daughter from the mother—he that loveth father or mother more than Me is not worthy of Me."

A terrible responsibility rests on the conscience of some parents, who, through selfishness or misguided love, succeed in preventing their children from following the call of God, and unscrupulously withhold from Him those He is drawing to Himself.

They may have the satisfaction of keeping a little longer with them those to whom they have given birth, but they must answer one day to their Judge for the immense good they have hindered, and the souls of those lost through their fault. Though it meant a big sacrifice, even a serious loss, no right-minded father would dream for a moment of forbidding a marriage which would bring to his child joy and good fortune; why then interfere with that holy alliance, made in heaven, which means far greater happiness?

St. Ambrose asks is it just that a young girl should have less liberty in choosing God for her Spouse than she has in selecting an earthly one. To the mother of a family who opposes the religious vocation of her daughter one might say:"You married, and you did well. Had you been forced to enter a convent, would you have done it?"

4. *"I could do more good in the world."*—In a very exceptional case, and under circumstances not likely to be realised, this might be true, but such a statement generally shows a want of realisation of the immense advantages of religious life, and the merit which comes from living under vows.

Would St. Francis, St. Dominic, or St. Ignatius have done more for God's glory had they led the life of pious laymen, and would not the world have been poorer and heaven emptier if Nano Nagle, Catherine Macauley or Mary Aikenhead had refused the grace offered them?

5. *"Good people are wanted in the world."*—But does God want ME there? If so, why did He give me a call to leave it? Surely I must take it for granted that He knows what is best for me and for His glory, and blindly follow His voice.

Père Olivaint, one of the Jesuit Martyrs of the Commune, answers the objection of a young man who wished to remain in the world as follows:"My parents have plans for my future…. But what does God want? In that position which is offered to me men will hold me in great esteem….But God? My natural taste moves me in that direction. But God? I shall certainly be able to save my soul in the world….True, but does God wish that you should save it there?"

Granting that I have a clear vocation to the religious life, where I shall be far better able and more fitted to work for the welfare of my neighbour, I cannot persuade myself that I could do more good by going against the Will of God.

6. *"I may be unhappy in the convent."*—Is the world, then, such an earthly paradise, so full of love, peace and happiness that no sorrow is to be found there? Religious may have much to suffer, days of trial and desolation to be endured, the grinding monotony of a never-changing round of duties to be bravely faced, day by day, yet with St. Paul they can exclaim: "I superabound with joy in the midst of my tribulations."

"Father," said an old Trappist monk, "I have so much consolation here amid all our austerities I fear I shall have none in the next world."

"One evening in winter," writes the Little Flower, "I was about my lowly occupation; it was cold and dark. Suddenly I heard the harmony of several musical instruments outside the convent, and pictured to myself a richly furnished, brilliantly-lit drawing-room, resplendent with gilding and decorations; young ladies, tastefully dressed were sitting there and paying each other many a vain compliment. Then I looked on the poor invalid I was tending. For the music I had her complaints; for the gilded drawing-room, the brick walls of an austere convent, lighted only by a feeble glimmer. The contrast was exceedingly sweet. The dim light of earthly joys was denied me, but the light of God shone all around. No, I would not have bartered those ten minutes taken by my deed of charity for ten thousand years of worldly diversions."

"Here in Carmel," she adds, "a prey to bodily and spiritual anguish, I am happier than I was in the world; yes, happier even than in my home, and by my beloved father's side."

7. *"Perhaps I never had a vocation."*—Many persons have been tried by great doubts about their vocation, sometimes fearing they had deceived themselves, and that it would be impossible for them to secure their salvation in the religious state. All sweetness and devotion seems to have vanished; everything is wearisome, prayer, spiritual reading, even recreation, a clear sign, they think, that God never wished them to enter!

Theologians, and at their head St. Liguori, lay it down as a principle that even if one should enter religion without a vocation and persevere through the novitiate, God would certainly give one at the moment of pronouncing one's vows. To hesitate or doubt when that step has been taken would be treason: "He who puts his hand to the plough and looks back, is not worthy of Me." Moreover, that repugnance and even dislike, which some suffer from during the whole of their religious life, is not a sign of want of vocation, if they persevere; God is only trying their fidelity to increase their merit.

8. *"Wait! Wait! Wait!"*

"If I were you I would not be in such a hurry."—But Jesus would not let the young man remain even to bury his father: "Let the dead bury their dead," He said, "and come thou and follow Me—make haste and tarry not."

"You do not know the world."—I know it is my worst foe, the friend and helper of my deadly enemy, Satan, and a danger I should fear and fly from.

"You are too young, wait a while."—Should I wait till the foul breath of the world has tarnished the beauty of the lily of my soul, which God loves for its spotless purity and wants for Himself? "It is well for a man who has borne the yoke from his youth."

Advantages of Religious Life[4]

Within the limits of a small pamphlet it would be impossible to give even an outline of the advantages of the religious state, and the heavenly favours enjoyed by those who are called to such a life. "What a glorious kingdom of the Holy Ghost is the religious state!" writes Father Meschler, S.J. "It is like an island of peace and calm in the middle of the fleeting, changing, restless flood of this earthly life. It is like a garden planted by God and blessed with the fat of the land and the dew of heavenly consolation. It is like a lofty mountain where the last echoes of this world are still, and the first sounds of a blessed eternity are heard. What peace, what happiness, purity and holiness has it shed over the face of the earth."

Nor is this to be wondered at, since God is never outdone in generosity, rewarding the sacrifices made in obedience to His call with a lavish hand.

"Peter said to him: Behold, we have left all things, and have followed Thee: what, therefore, shall we have? And Jesus said to them: You shall receive a hundredfold and possess life everlasting."

"Taste and see how sweet the Lord is," says the Psalmist, for only those who have experience of the happiness, peace and contentment of the cloister realise fully the truth of the Saviour's words: "Mary hath chosen the better part." The present writer

---

[4] The reader is referred to the excellent little book by St. Alphonsus Liguori, *Choice of a State of Life* (Bassi, Wellington Quay, Dublin. Two Parts, 2d.), where the famous saying of St. Bernard is well developed: "A religious lives more purely, falls more rarely, rises more speedily, walks more cautiously, is bedewed more frequently with heavenly graces, rests more securely, dies more confidently, is purged more quickly, and rewarded more abundantly."

could quote the heartfelt words of gratitude to God from many a soul for the grace of their vocation. One who had to suffer much in breaking the ties which bound her to the world and home, writes: "I seem to be slowly awakening from a long dream. I am so very happy I do not know if I am myself or some one else. How can I ever thank God enough for bringing me here?"

St. Jerome compares religious, who have left the world, to the Israelites delivered from the bondage of Egypt, and says God has shown great love for them in exchanging their hard slavery for the sweet liberty of the children of God.

A.—Its Happiness

Many caricatures have been painted of monks and nuns, depicting them as a merry, jovial crew, rejoicing in the good things of this world, but no artist has ever yet drawn a religious community as a collection of sad-faced, melancholy beings. The very atmosphere of a convent is joy and tranquility, its inmates bright and cheerful; for, safe from the storms and troubles of the world and the insatiable desire for wealth, free from the cares, the anxieties, of a home and family, protected by the mantle of a loving charity from the disputes, the quarrels and petty jealousies of life, they have at last found true happiness, which consists in peace of soul and contentment of heart.

The world may boast of many things, but it cannot claim to give happiness to its followers. One who had the means of gratifying every craving, Solomon, sadly exclaimed: "Whatsoever my eyes desired, I refused them not, and I withheld not my heart from enjoying every pleasure, but I saw in all things only vanity and vexation of spirit, except to love God and serve Him alone."

The life of a religious, like that of every other human being, must be a warfare to the end; they have their crosses and tribulations, and God, in order to sanctify them, often sends great trials and interior sufferings, yet through it all, deep down in the soul they feel the presence of Christ's most precious gift: "My peace I leave you, My peace I give you," that peace of heart, "a continual feast," which the world knows not of, nor can earthly pleasures bestow.

Hence St. Lawrence Justinian says: "Almighty God has designedly concealed the happiness of religious life, because if it were known all would relinquish the world and fly to religion."

"An earthly Paradise," says St. Mary Magdalen of Pazzi; and St. Scholastica, "If men knew the peace which religious enjoy in retirement, the entire world would become one great convent."

Secure in the possession of God, rejoicing in the promise of a glorious eternity, is it any wonder that those who have left all to follow Christ should find "His yoke sweet and His burden light"? The writer of *Recit d'une Soeur* sums up well this picture of true religious life in these words: "Happiness in heaven purchased by happiness on earth."

B.—Its Holiness

Spiritual writers say that life in religion surpasses all others, because it removes obstacles to perfection and consecrates one, in the most perfect manner, to God.

The world, with its round of amusements and distractions is the deadly enemy of piety, and even the best disposed persons find it hard not to be influenced by the prevailing spirit of indifference to spiritual things, or unaffected by so much careless, if not downright evil, example around them. Many a holy soul hungers for prayer and recollection, only to find that the cares of a family, the calls of social duties, the unavoidable visits and entertainment, encroach far on the limited time they can give to God.

In religion, on the other hand, care of the soul is the first and most important duty, its advancement and perfection the great business of life.

By a wise economy of time, religious, in spite of many other occupations, can devote four or five hours a day to meditation, prayer, visits to the Blessed Sacrament, and the recitation of the Office, so well distributed that no burden is felt.

His Rules and the voice of Obedience make known to him the Will of God, which he could never be certain of in the world; they protect him from a multitude of dangerous temptation, shutting out in great measure the possibility of sin; the company of so many chosen souls, their generous example and saintly lives, spur him on to nobler things; saved from all worldly anxieties, he can give his whole heart to the service and love of God, leading a life which is an earnest, if humble, imitation of his Lord and Master Jesus Christ.

"O Lord," cries out holy David, "a single day in Thy house is worth a thousand in the courts of sinners." "I hold it for certain," says St. Alphonsus, "that the greatest number of the vacant thrones of the fallen Seraphim will be occupied by souls sanctified in the religious state. Among the sixty persons canonised during the last century there were only five who did not belong to religious orders."

C.— "The Triple Cord"—The Vows

But that which constitutes the essence of religious life, and gives to it such merit, is the observance of the three vows of Evangelical

Perfection—Poverty, Chastity and Obedience. A vow is a solemn promise made to God, after serious deliberation and having fully grasped its responsibilities, by which the soul engages to perform something, under pain of sin, which is better to do than to omit.

It is certain that it is more perfect and more agreeable to God to do a good work, after having obliged ourselves to do it by vow, than to do it freely without this obligation. For, as St. Thomas says, an act of perfect virtue is always of itself more excellent than that of a lesser virtue. Thus, an act of charity is more meritorious than an act of mortification, since charity is a more perfect virtue than the virtue of penance. After the theological virtues of Faith, Hope and Charity, the most perfect of all is the virtue of Religion, by which we worship God; a vow is an act of this the noblest of all the moral virtues, the Virtue of Religion, and by it all the actions performed in virtue of the vows are elevated to the dignity of acts of religion, giving them not only much greater value in the eyes of God and imparting to the will constancy and firmness in well-doing, but immensely increasing the holiness of the person, since from each action he reaps a double reward, the merit of the act of virtue, and the merit of the act of religion, imparted by the vow.

Of all the vows that can be made, the three of the religious state are the noblest and the best. The perfection of a Christian consists in renouncing the cupidities of life, in trampling on the world, in breaking all ties that hold him captive, and in being bound and united to God by perfect charity. The three great obstacles that prevent him from acquiring this perfection are, according to St. John, the concupiscence of the eyes for riches, the concupiscence of the flesh for the pleasures of the senses, and the pride of life for seeking after honours. The vow of poverty destroys the first, the vow of chastity the second, and that of obedience the third.

By these vows man makes of himself a perfect sacrifice to God, he offers himself as a holocaust to His glory, surrendering into His hands, for ever, not only all earthly possessions that he has or might have, but even gives up his liberty and will, the most perfect immolation a human being can make.

Seeing how pleasing is this lifelong sacrifice to God, the Fathers of the Church, St. Jerome, St. Bernard, the Angelic Doctor and many others, have always called religious profession a "Second Baptism," by which the guilt and punishment due for past sins is entirely remitted.

"A religious lives more happily and dies more confidently," wrote St. Bernard; and well he may, for he knows that the three vows which bound him for ever to the service of his Master have washed away all trace of a sinful past, that the evil deeds of his life, be they as numerous as the sands on the sea-shore, with all the dreadful consequences they brought with them, have been blotted out by the recording angel, and that his soul is as pure and spotless as when first the waters of baptism made him the heir of heaven: "Greater love than this no man hath," said the Saviour, "that a man lay down his life for his friends," and, adds the Apostle: "Charity (the love of God) covereth a multitude of sins." By the daily crucifixion of his life, the religious makes this offering of all that is dear to him into the hands of his Friend and Master, a martyrdom far more painful than that of blood, but one which he knows will win for him a glorious crown.

One can easily understand, then, the determination of those who for one reason or another have been obliged to leave a religious house to enter again. Disappointment, delays, even refusal, seem but to increase their longing to give themselves to God, for they have learned in the convent the beauty and grandeur of a life which is "All for Jesus," they have tasted its sweetness and realised the possibilities of immense holiness within its walls, and, like Isabella of France, who refused the hand of the Emperor Frederick to become a humble nun, they exclaim: "A spouse of Jesus Christ is far more than even an Empress."

The Harvest of Souls

In the preceding pages we have seen briefly the nature and obligation of a vocation, and glanced at a few of its privileges and advantages. Yet some, even among Catholics, may be found to ask what need is there for so many priests and nuns?

Long ago, while yet the Saviour trod this earth, we read that once He sat by the well-side, weary from His journeyings. As He paused to rest, His gaze fell upon the waving cornfields stretching far out of sight, the ears bending under their load of countless, tiny seeds, each bearing its germ of life. To the eyes of His soul, devoured with a burning zeal, it was an image of the vast multitude of human beings He had come to save, of the souls of those with whom He lived and the myriads who would follow Him. Silently He looks at the solitary husbandman, sickle in hand, slowly gathering the sheaves of golden corn, then sadly turning to the disciples, He says, with a hidden meaning in His words: "The harvest indeed is great, but the labourers are few. Pray ye, therefore, the Lord of the harvest that He send labourers into His harvest."

The words died away, but their echo has never ceased to sound. "The harvest is great, but the labourers are few." Turn where we will, in no matter what part of the globe, and there we shall see still the harvest of souls, waiting to be garnered into the Master's granaries.

"Send me half a million priests," writes a Jesuit missioner from India, "and I promise to find them abundant work at once."

"For the love of God come out to us. I have come across millions of men here in Africa who need but to hear Our Lord's words and deeds to become so many good and happy Christians."

Another, as he gazes at the teeming Chinese population around him, exclaims: "The ten thousand catechumens of my district would be a hundred thousand tomorrow if there were priests and nuns enough to instruct and receive them."

"The harvest indeed is great"—a total Pagan population in the world of 995,000,000 (nine hundred and ninety-five millions), or eight out of every thirteen of the human race, who have never heard the Name of God, each with an immortal soul looking for salvation. America, on the authority of Archbishop Ireland, with its forty thousand converts in one year; England, registering, at the last census, twenty million of her people as having "no religion," while from every town and village of our own land comes the cry for more Brothers, Priests and Nuns to labour in the fields "white with the harvest."

"Pray ye, therefore," still pleads the Saviour from the tabernacle, as He gazes on the vast work yet to be done, "pray ye the Lord that He send labourers, many and zealous, into His harvest."

An Appeal

Boys and girls of Ireland, with your young lives so full of promise opening out before you, have you no nobler ideals, no loftier ambition, than to spend your days in pleasure and amusement, while your brothers and your sisters look appealingly to you for help? Lift up your eyes and see the harvest awaiting you, the most glorious work ever given man to do—the saving of immortal souls.

The day of Ireland's greatest glory was the time when the land was covered with a golden network of schools and monasteries; when her missioners and nuns were to be found in every clime and country; when every tenth Irishman and woman was consecrated to God and His service. "If our country would be born again," wrote Thomas Francis Meagher, "she must be baptised once more in the old Irish holy well." This is the work that lies before you, the work God looks to you to do— strengthening the Faith that St. Patrick left us, preaching the truth to an unbelieving world, sacrificing yourselves, as your ancestors did before you, leaving home and friends, and, for the sake of God and Ireland, giving your life that others may be saved.

A vocation is, indeed, the gift of God, but through love for the souls whom He longs to save, gladly would He bestow it on many more, if only they would listen to His voice or ask Him for this treasure.

Are you one, dear reader, at whose heart Jesus has long been knocking, perhaps in vain, inviting, pleading, urging? "The Master is here and calls for you"; He has need of you for His work. Follow Him bravely and trustfully, you will never regret it. But if you have not yet heard that voice, then remember His words: "Ask and you shall receive"; ask Him for a vocation, not once but daily, ask confidently, perseveringly, for He has pledged His word to hear you, so that you, also, may share the happiness of those who serve the Lord, and that "your joy"— like theirs—"may be full."

"One thing I have asked of the Lord, this will I seek after, that I may dwell in the house of the Lord all the days of my life."—Ps. XXVI. 4.

The Peoples' Prayer for Their Priests

O loving Heart of Jesus! deign to listen to the pleading supplication of Thy people for the sanctification of their pastors. O Heart of Love! teach them to love Thee as Thou desirest; make them holy, make them pure, make them prudent, make them wise, make them "be all things to all men" after Thy divine example. They are the guardians of Thy sacred Flesh and Blood: Oh! make them faithful to this holy trust. Give them excessive reverence for Thy pure Body and a longing thirst for Thy precious Blood, so that having tasted of Its sweetness they may be sanctified, strengthened and purified in the consuming flame of divine love.

O dearest Jesus! do not refuse our humble prayer. Look down with love on Thy priests; fill them with burning zeal for the conversion of sinners; keep unstained their anointed hands which daily touch Thy Immaculate Body; keep unsullied their lips purpled with Thy Precious Blood; keep pure and unearthly a heart sealed with the sublime marks of Thy glorious Priesthood; bless their labours with abundant fruit, and may those to whom they have ministered on earth be one day their joy and consolation in Heaven.

Eucharistic Heart of Jesus, model of the priestly heart, give us holy priests. Amen.

The Choice of a State of Life

PRAYER

(Indulgence, 300 days, once a day. Pius X, May 6, 1905)

O my God, Thou who art the God of wisdom and of counsel, Thou who readest in my heart the sincere will to please Thee alone, and to govern myself with regard to my choice of a state of life, entirely in conformity with Thy most holy desire; grant me, by the intercession of the most blessed Virgin, my Mother, and of my holy patrons, especially of St. Joseph and St. Aloysius, the grace to know what state I ought to choose; and when to embrace it, so that in it I may be able to pursue and increase Thy glory, work out my salvation, and merit that heavenly reward which Thou hast promised to those who do Thy holy Will. Amen.

*Synopsis of the Rubrics &
Ceremonies of Holy Mass*

Nihil obstat: F. Thos. Bergh, O.S.B., *Censor Deputatus*
Imprimatur: Edm. Can. Surmont, *Vicarius Generalis*
Westmonasteri, Die 8 Marti, 1914

A.M.D.G.

---

*Recepti et approbati Catholicae Ecclesiae ritus, qui in
minimis etiam sine peccato negligi, omitti aut mutari
haud possunt, peculiari studio ac diligentia serventur.*

—Roman Synod, 1725

I. Preparation

1. See that the Missal is properly marked.
2. Wash hands, saying prayer, *Da, Domine, virtutem.*
3. Before vesting, prepare Chalice—Opening of Burse to be turned towards Priest.
4. Leave Ciborium, key of Tabernacle, etc., on altar. Nothing should be carried on top of Chalice.
5. When vesting, kiss cross on amice, maniple, and stole.
6. Bow to Cross and take holy water when leaving sacristy, eyes cast down. If sacristy is behind altar, go out by Epistle side and return by Gospel.
7. If necessary to pass the High Altar or any altar where Blessed Sacrament is reserved, genuflect on one knee without uncovering head. If not carrying Chalice, head is uncovered.

8. Passing Blessed Sacrament exposed, or during the Consecration, or giving of Communion, kneel down on both knees—Uncover head. Bow slightly—Put on biretta before rising from knees. When not carrying Chalice, head is uncovered at once if Blessed Sacrament is exposed, or Communion being given.

9. Slight bow of head without uncovering to Bishop or to any priest going to celebrate or returning. Give precedence to him who has celebrated.

10. Arrived at altar, give biretta to server—Gentlect *in plano*, not on first step (profound bow to Cross if Blessed Sacrament is not reserved)—Right foot first, ascend steps.

11. Place Chalice towards Gospel Side—Unfold Corporal fully —Place Chalice in centre.

12. Hands joined before breast, palm to palm, fingers extended straight together, slightly pointing upwards, right thumb over left. Walk slowly to Epistle corner—Open Missal. NOTE.—The hands are kept joined in this manner during the whole of Mass, unless otherwise stated.

13. Return to centre—Slight bow to Cross—Turn round towards Epistle side—Descend steps—Hands joined, eyes lowered.

II. Beginning of Mass

1. Hands joined—Genuflect on lowest step (profound reverence to Cross if Blessed Sacrament is not reserved).

2. *In nomine Patris* (clear tone of voice).—Left hand under breast, make sign of cross.

3. *Judica me Deus.*—Omitted in Dead Mass.

4. *Gloria Patri.*—Bow head only.

5. *Adjutorium nostrum.*—Sign of cross, left hand under breast.

6. *Confiteor.*—Hands joined before breast— Bow profoundly till server has finished *Misereatur.*
7. At words *vobis fratres* and *vos fratres* no inclination to server, as at High Mass.
8. *Mea culpa.*—Left hand under breast— Strike breast with fingers of right hand joined and extended (hand is not clenched).
9. *Indulgentiam.*—Left hand under breast—Sign of cross.
10. *Deus tu conversus.*—Moderate inclination of head and shoulders.
11. *Oremus.*—Stand erect—Extend hands, and rejoin without raising them.

III. The Introit

1. *Aufer a nobis* (secretly).—Hands joined—Ascend steps, right foot first.
2. *Oramus te, Domine.*—Bowing moderately, place joined hands on edge of altar, so that tips of little fingers touch front edge.
3. *Quorum reliquiæ.*—Kiss altar in centre, not at side—Hands placed flat on altar, outside Corporal.
4. Standing at Missal, make sign of cross, left hand under breast. (In Dead Mass Sign of cross is made over book.)
5. *Gloria Patri*—Turn slightly—Bow bead to Cross—Eyes not raised.
6. *Kyrie Eleison.*—At centre of altar, and not before reaching it.

IV. Gloria in Excelsis

1. *Gloria.* Hands separated in straight line, raised to height of shoulders—At *Deo* joined again and head bowed—Eyes not raised to Cross.

2. Head (not shoulders) bowed at *Adoramus Te, Gratias agimus, Jesu Christe* (twice), *Suscipe deprecationem*.
3. *Cum Sancto Spiritu.*—Left hand under breast—Sign of cross.
4. *Amen.*—Hands not rejoined, but placed flat on altar, outside Corporal—Kiss altar in centre.
5. *Dominus vobiscum.*—Hands joined, turn round by Epistle side—Eyes cast down—Extend to shoulders and rejoin hands in straight line without elevating them—turn back same way.

V. The Prayers

1. *Oremus.*—Turn slightly and bow head to Cross, extending and rejoining hands. During the Prayers, hands held extended, so as not to exceed the height and width of the shoulders, palms facing each other, fingers joined, pointing upwards.
2. At Holy Name, head bowed to Cross.
3. At name of Saint of the day, or Blessed Virgin, or Pope, head bowed to Missal.
4. *Per Dominum.*—Hands joined and kept thus till *Amen*.
5. *Jesum Christum.*—Head bowed to Cross. If prayer concludes with *Qui vivis* or *Qui tecum*, hands not joined till *in unitate*—No bow made to Cross.
   NOTE.—The conclusion, *Per Dominum*, etc., is only used with the first and last prayer.

VI. The Epistle

1. Palms of hands rest on Missal during the Epistle, or book may be held with both hands.

2. If genuflection has to be made, hands placed flat on altar.
3. *Munda cor meum.*—Standing at centre of altar. Eyes raised for a moment to Cross—Bow profoundly—Hands joined between breast and altar, but not touching altar.
4. In Dead Mass, *Jube Domine* and *Dominus sit* omitted.

VII. The Gospel

1. *Dominus vobiscum.*—Hands joined before breast—Missal placed with opening towards centre of altar.
2. *Sequentia sancti Evangelii.*—Left hand on Missal, make sign of cross with right thumb on book—Left hand under breast, sign of cross with right thumb on forehead, mouth, and breast, distributing words with actions.
3. Hands rejoined—Head bowed to the book at the name of Jesus, of Mary, or of Saint of the day.
4. Genuflection also made to Missal.
5. *Per evangelica dicta.*—Missal raised with both hands—Kissed where signed in the beginning of Gospel.

VIII. Credo

1. Hands extended, raised to height of shoulders and rejoined at breast. Head bowed to Cross without raising eyes.
2. *Jesum Christum.*—Bow head.
3. *Et incarnatus.*—Hands flat on altar, outside Corporal, genuflect.
4. *Et homo factus est.*—These words said with knee on ground—Head not bowed.
5. *Simul adoratur.*—Bow head.
6. *Et vitam venturi sæculi.*—Said while making sign of cross—Left hand under breast.

7. *Amen.*—Hands not rejoined, but placed flat on altar, outside Corporal—Kiss altar in centre—*Dominus vobiscum* as before.

IX. The Offertory

1. *Oremus.*—Hands extended and rejoined in straight line—Head bowed to Cross.
2. *Offertorium.*—Prayer read with hands joined.
3. Veil folded, left outside Corporal on Epistle side.
4. Left hand on altar—Place Chalice outside Corporal towards Epistle side—Pall upright against corner of Chart, or left on Veil—With right hand take Paten—Hold with both hands, thumbs and index-fingers round edge, others joined underneath—Raise over middle of Corporal, breast high.
5. *Suscipe, sancte Pater* (secretly).—Eyes raised to Cross, then fixed on Host.
6. Prayer ended, lower Paten to about four inches from Corporal—Form sign of cross, each arm nine inches long—Incline Paten away from self so that Host may slip into front fold on Corporal.
7. Left hand on altar—Place Paten halfway under Corporal on Epistle side.
8. Hands joined, walk to Epistle corner—Take Chalice at knob with left hand—Wipe inside slightly with Purificator held in right—Hold end of Purificator with left thumb on knob—Pour wine into Chalice, *nihil dicens*.
9. *Deus qui humanæ.*—Sign of cross over water (omitted in Dead Mass).
10. *Per hujus aquæ.*—Some drops of water added to wine (Chalice should not be struck with spoon).

11. *Jesus Christus.*—Join hands—Bow head to Cross—While finishing prayer, wipe inside of Chalice with Purificator round index-finger of right hand.

12. Walk to centre—Hands joined holding Purificator—Place it over Paten.

13. Left hand on altar, outside Corporal— Take Chalice by knob with right, thumb in front, fingers behind—Place left fingers under foot of Chalice—Raise so that top of Chalice may not be higher than eyes.

14. *Offerimus tibi.*—Eyes on Cross during the whole prayer— Make Cross with Chalice above second fold of Corporal (not over Host)—Place in centre of Corporal—Cover with Pall, keeping fingers of left hand on foot of Chalice,
NOTE.—When covering or uncovering the Chalice, the left-hand fingers are always placed on the base of the Chalice to steady it.

15. *In spiritu humilitatis.*—Incline moderately—Place joined hands on edge of altar so that tips of little fingers touch front edge.

16. *Veni Sanctificator*—Standing upright, separate hands, raise to height of shoulders, rejoin, and lower again— Raise Eyes to heaven, not to Cross.

17. *Et Bene†dic.*—Sign of cross over both Chalice and Host— Left hand on altar, outside Corporal.

X. Lavabo

1. *Lavabo inter innocentes.*—Wash tips of forefingers and thumbs—Turn, facing altar, while finishing Psalm.

2. Left hand on altar when handing lavabo cloth to server.

3. *Gloria Patri.*—Bow head to Cross— Eyes not raised (*Gloria* omitted in Dead Mass).

4. Hands joined, walk slowly to centre, finishing *Gloria.*

5. *Suscipe, sancta Trinitas.*—Raise eyes to Cross—Moderately inclined—Hands joined, fingers touching edge of altar.

6. Hands flat on altar, outside Corporal—Kiss centre.

7. *Orate fratres* (moderate tone of voice).— Hands joined— Turn towards people by Epistle side—Eyes cast down— Extend and rejoin hands in straight line without elevating them—Turn back immediately by Gospel side, finishing, secretly, *Ut meum ac vestrum sacrificium.* At end of server's response, *Amen* (in secret).

8. Hands extended, palms facing, read the Secrets—*Oremus* not said.

    Amen (secretly) after first prayer only.

XI. The Preface

1. *Per omnia* (clear tone of voice).—Hands flat on altar, outside Corporal.

2. *Sursum corda.*—Raise hands to height of shoulders, palms opposite each other, fingers joined and straight.

3. *Gratias agamus.*—Join hands in front of breast.

4. *Deo nostro.*—Raise eyes to Cross—Bow head.

5. *Vere dignum.*—Hands held extended during Preface.

6. *Sanctus* (lower tone of voice).—Join hands—Moderately inclined—Hands held before breast, not touching altar.

7. *Benedictus.*—Stand erect—Sign of cross—Left hand under breast.

8. *Hosanna in excelsis.*—Hands joined.

XII. The Canon

NOTE.—When one hand is used to turn the pages of the Missal, the other is placed flat on the altar, outside the Corporal before the Consecration, on the Corporal afterwards.

1. *Te igitur.*—Hands joined before breast— Separate, elevate a little, and rejoin them—Raise eyes to Cross—Bow profoundly—Tips of little fingers touching outside edge of altar—Prayers said secretly.

2. *Petimus.*—Hands flat on altar, outside Corporal—Kiss centre of altar—Rise and rejoin hands.

3. *Hæc † dona,*   { Three crosses over both Chalice and
   Hæc † munera,   { Host—Left hand on altar, outside
   Hæc † sancta   { Corporal.

   NOTE.—The sign of the cross should be made slowly, in straight lines of equal length and breadth (about nine inches each way).

4. *In primis.*—Hands not rejoined, but held extended, so as not to exceed height and width of shoulders, palms facing, fingers upright.

5. *Papa nostro N.*—Bow head to Missal.

6. *Antistite nostro N.*—Head not bowed.

XIII. Commemoration of Living

1. *Memento, Domine.*—Slowly raise and join hands, holding them near face, fingers pointing upwards.

2. *Et omnium circumstantium.*—Hands lowered and extended.

3. *Communicantes.*—Bow head to Missal at *Mariae*, or name of Saint whose feast is commemorated.

NOTE.—If a statue of Our Blessed Lady is over the altar, the inclination at the name of Mary is made to it, and not towards the Missal.

4. *Jesu Christi.*—Bow head to Cross.
5. *Per eumdem Christum.*—Hands joined—Head not bowed.

XIV. Hanc Igitur

1. Keeping right thumb crossed over left, open hands and hold them flat over the Chalice, so that tips of fingers will reach as far as middle of Pall, not resting on it.
2. *Per Christum.*—Rejoin hands and draw back to breast.
3. *Bene†dictam, adscrip†tam, ra†tam.*—Left hand on altar, outside Corporal—Three crosses over both Chalice and Host.
4. *Cor†pus et San†guis.*—Lowering right hand slightly, make cross over Host only, then over Chalice only—Rejoin hands before breast.
5. *Jesu Christi.*—Bow head to Cross.

XV. Consecration of Host

1. *Qui Pridie*—Wipe thumbs and forefingers slightly on Corporal.
2. *Accepit panem.*—Raise Host by pressing with left forefinger on its edge—Take Host with forefinger and thumb of right hand, holding it on opposite side with left thumb and forefinger—Other three fingers extended and joined behind—Hold in this manner about nine inches over Corporal.
3. *Elevatis oculis.*—Raise eyes to heaven, not to Cross—Lower eyes at once.
4. *Tibi gratias agens.*—Bow head slightly.

5. *Bene†dixit.*—Make sign of cross over Host with right hand, holding it between left thumb and forefinger—Hand not resting on altar.

6. *Fregit deditque.*—Hold Host, as before, with both hands.

7. *Ex hoc omnes.*—Having finished these words, lean forward with elbows resting on front of altar, holding Host with both hands, not touching Corporal—Pronounce words of Consecration *secretly.*

"Hoc est enim Corpus Meum."

8. Holding Host between forefingers and thumbs, place hands on Corporal as far as the wrists—Slowly, with great reverence, genuflect to ground.
   NOTE.—Many Rubricists say the head should be bowed slightly at the adoration of the Host and Chalice, but never during the other genuflections.

9. Stand erect—Raise Host with both hands, in straight line over Corporal, *so that It may be seen by the people*— Eyes on Host the whole time. Care should be taken that the Host be not held outside the limits of the Corporal.

10. Without any perceptible pause, lower Host, still holding It with *both* hands—Place on Corporal—Genuflect slowly to ground.
    NOTE.—Thumb and forefinger of both hands remain joined till the ablution of fingers.

XVI. Consecration of Chalice

1. *Simili modo.*—Left fingers on foot of Chalice—Remove Pall with right— Purify thumb and forefinger by rubbing together over Chalice.

2. *Accipiens.*—Take knob of Chalice with thumbs and index-fingers of both hands joined in front, the others behind it—Raise Chalice a little, and replace on Corporal—Arms not resting on altar.

3. *In sanctas.*—Hold Chalice till end of prayer.

4. *Tibi gratias agens.*—Bow head to consecrated Host.

5. *Bene†dixit.*—Sign of cross over Chalice with right hand—Left still holding knob—Hold Chalice, as before, with both hands.

6. *Ex eo omnes.*—Rest elbows on altar—Hold Chalice with right hand at knob—Three last fingers of left under its foot—Raise Chalice a little so that hands will not touch the Corporal. Pronounce words of Consecration *secretly*.

"HIC EST ENIM CALIX."

7. *Hæc quotiescumgue.*—Replace Chalice in centre of Corporal—Both hands flat on Corporal—Genuflect slowly and reverently to ground.

8. On rising, take Chalice by the knob with right hand—Left fingers supporting foot—Raise in straight line over Corporal, so as to be seen by people—Without any notable pause, replace on altar—Eyes all the time fixed on Chalice.

9. Cover with Pall—Last three fingers of left hand on foot of Chalice—Genuflect slowly to ground.

XVII. After the Consecration

NOTE.—Till after the ablution of the fingers, the hands, when resting on the altar, are placed upon the Corporal; thumb and forefinger joined.

1. *Unde et memores.*—Stand erect—Hands extended at height of shoulders, palms facing each other—Eyes on Missal.
2. *De tuis donis.*—Join hands before breast.
3. *Hostiam † puram,* 　 Left hand on Corporal—Make
   Hostiam † sanctam, 　 three crosses (about nine inches
   Hostiam † immaculatam 　 in length each way) slowly over
   　　　　　　　　 both Chalice and Host.
4. *Panem † sanctum.*—Cross over Host only.
5. *Calicem † salutis.*—Cross over Chalice only.
6. *Supra quæ.*—Hands are not rejoined, but extended at once, as before.
7. *Supplices te rogamus.*—Bow profoundly—Hold hands joined and resting on edge of altar, tips of little fingers touching front edge.
8. *Ex hac altaris participatione.*—Place both hands flat on Corporal—Kiss altar in centre—Rejoin hands.
9. *Cor†pus.*—Left hand on Corporal— Cross over Host only.
10. *San†guinem.*—Cross over Chalice only.
11. *Omni benedictione † celesti.*—Left hand under breast—Sign self with right, distributing words with actions.
12. *Per eumdem Christum.*—Join hands at breast—Head not bowed.

XVII. Commemoration of the Dead

1. *Memento.*—Separate hands slowly, in straight line—Rejoin at *In somno pacis*—Bow head slightly—Raise hands so that fingers nearly touch face— Eyes fixed on Host during the Commemoration.
2. *Ipsis Domine.*—Raise head—Hands extended as before.

3. *Per eumdem Christum.*—Rejoin hands—Bow head.
   NOTE.—This is the only occasion on which the head is bowed at these words.
4. *Nobis quoque peccatoribus* (moderate tone of voice).—Left hand on Corporal—Strike breast with tips of fingers.
5. *Famulis tuis.*—Hands extended.
6. *Per Christum.*—Join hands before breast —No *Amen*.
7. *Sancti†ficas,*
   Vivi†ficas, } Three crosses over both Chalice and Host
   Bene†dicis —Left hand on Corporal.
8. *Et præstas nobis.*—Left fingers on foot of Chalice—Remove Pall—Both hands flat on Corporal—Genuflect.
9. *Per ip†sum,* { Holding Chalice at knob with left hand,
   Et cum ip†so, } make three crosses with Host over mouth
   Et in ip†so of Chalice, not passing rim.
10. *Patri † Omnipotenti,* { Two crosses with Host over Corpo-
    Spiritus † Sancti } ral only, between Chalice and edge
    of altar.
11. *Omnis honor et gloria.*—Hold Host over Chalice, fingers resting on rim—Raise Chalice a little with left hand.
12. Replace Chalice and Host on altar—Purify fingers over Cup—Rejoin finger and thumb—Cover Chalice with Pall—Left fingers on foot—Genuflect—Hands flat on Corporal.

XIX. Pater Noster

1. *Per omnia* (clear voice).—Hands fat on Corporal.
2. *Oremus.*—Join hands before breast—Bow head to Host.
3. *Pater noster.*—Extend hands—Eyes on Host.

4. *Amen* (secretly).—Remove Paten from under Corporal—Wipe with Purificator, which is left on Epistle side.

5. *Libera nos quesumus.*—Hold Paten between fore and middle finger—Edge resting on altar, outside Corporal—Concave part inwards—Left hand flat on Corporal.

6. *Da propitius.*—Left hand under breast—Sign self with Paten—Kiss inside edge.

7. *Ut ope.*—Put Paten under Host, using left forefinger to push It into centre—Lean Paten on foot of Chalice.

8. Uncover Chalice—Left fingers on foot—Genuflect—Move Host towards right edge of Paten with left forefinger.

9. *Per eumdem Dominum.*—Hold Host with right hand over Chalice—With finger and thumb of both hands break Host down the centre.

10. *Jesum Christum.*—Bow head.

11. *Qui tecum.* Place right half of Host on Paten—With right hand break off a small piece from other half.

12. *In unitate.*—Place left half of Host on Paten beside other—Hold Particle in right hand over Chalice.

13. *Per omnia* (audible voice).—Hold Chalice at knob with left hand, thumb and forefinger in front, other three behind.

14. *Pax † Domini sit † semper vobis†cum.*—Three crosses with Particle over Chalice from rim to rim.

15. *Hæc commixtio.*—Let Particle fall into Chalice.

16. *Jesu Christi.*—Bow head.

17. *In vitam æternam. Amen.*—Purify thumbs and forefingers over Chalice—Cover with Pall—Left fingers on foot—Genuflect.

XX. Agnus Dei

1. *Agnus Dei* (audible voice).—Hands joined before breast, but not touching altar—Body moderately inclined.
2. *Miserere nobis.*—Left hand on Corporal—Strike breast with tips of last three fingers.

   NOTE.—While saying the second and third *Agnus Dei*, the right hand may rest on the Corporal, or be moved slowly to and fro.

   In Mass for the Dead the breast is not struck at *Dona eis requiem.*
3. *Domine Jesu Christe.*—Body moderately inclined—Hands joined—Tips of little fingers touching front edge of altar—Eyes fixed on Host.

   NOTE. —In Dead Mass the first prayer is omitted.
4. *Panem cælestem accipiam.*—Hands flat on Corporal—Genuflect—Move both parts of Host towards edge of Paten with right forefinger—With left hand hold Host so that the two halves may not overlap, but form a circle—With right place Paten under Host, between middle and forefinger of left hand.

XXI. Domine non sum Dignus

1. *Domine non sum dignus* (moderate tone of voice).—Hold Host and Paten about four inches over Corporal—Left arm not resting on altar—Body slightly inclined—Strike breast with tips of right fingers.
2. *Ut intres sub tectum.*—Secretly.
3. *Corpus Domini.*—Stand erect—With right hand take both parts of Host, laying one over the other—Raise Host to height of eyes—Lower again, making sign of cross over Paten.

4. *Jesu Christi.*—Bow head.

5. *In vitam æternam. Amen.*—Lean elbows on altar—Body inclined—Paten under chin while receiving Sacred Species.

6. Place Paten on Corporal at foot of Chalice—Purify fingers over centre of Paten—Stand erect—Hands joined near face.

7. *Quid retribuam.*—Left fingers on foot of Chalice —Remove Pall—Genuflect—Take Paten between middle and forefinger of right hand and gather Particles on Corporal, which may be raised at side with left hand.

8. Hold Paten between middle and forefinger of left hand over Chalice—With right purify into Chalice.

9. *Calicem salutaris.*—Still holding Paten between fingers, rest left hand on Corporal—Take Chalice under knob with the three fingers of right.

10. *Sanguis Domini nostri.*—Raise Chalice till top is on level with eyes—Lower a little, making sign of cross—Left hand with Paten resting on altar.

11. *Jesu Christi.*—Bow head.

12. *In vitam æternam. Amen.*—Paten under chin—Consume Precious Blood, *unico haustu*, if possible—Chalice should not be turned upside down while doing so.

XXII. Purification of Chalice

1. *Quod ore sumpsimus.*—Paten between fingers, rest left hand in middle of Corporal—Hold Chalice towards Epistle corner, not touching altar—Consume wine with Paten under chin.

2. Place Paten on back part of Corporal, behind Chalice—Holding Chalice with both hands, thumbs and forefingers over Cup, carry to Epistle corner.

3. *Corpus tuum, Domine.*—Receive wine and water on fingers held over Chalice—Without removing fingers, place Chalice between Corporal and Purificator—Shake fingers slightly over Chalice—Take Purificator with right hand, place over left fingers, still in Chalice—Dry them while going to middle of altar.

4. While consuming ablutions, hold Purificator, folded over left forefinger, under chin—Place Chalice in centre of Corporal—Wipe lips with Purificator—Wipe whole of inside of Chalice.

5. Place Chalice with left hand outside Corporal on Gospel side—Fold and place Purificator over it—With right put on Paten and Pall.

6. Fold Corporal with both hands, beginning with fold nearest self—Place inside Burse, which is left flat on altar—Cover Chalice with Veil and Burse, and then place in centre of altar.

XXIII. Postconmmunion

1. Hands joined before breast, read prayers in a clear voice.

2. *Dominus vobiscum.*—Hands flat on altar —Kiss in centre— Turn round by Epistle side—Eyes cast down.

3. *Oremus.*—Turn a little and bow head to Cross—Extend hands—Rejoin—Extend again.
NOTE.—If there is more than one Postcommunion, the conclusion Per Dominum is used with the first and last only.

4. Close Missal, with opening towards middle of altar.

5. *Dominus vobiscum.*—Kiss altar in centre.

6. *Ite, missa est.*—Hands joined—Eyes lowered.

7. *Benedicamus Domino* or *Requiescant in pace* is said facing altar.

XXIV. Last Gospel

1. *Placeat Tibi.*—Hands joined—Little fingers touching front edge of altar—Body moderately inclined.
2. *Benedicat vos.*—Kiss altar in centre—Stand erect—Lift eyes to heaven, extend and raise hands, taking care not to exceed width and height of shoulders—Rejoin at breast—Bow head.
3. *Pater et Filius.*—Hands joined at breast—Eyes cast down—Turn round by Epistle side—Left hand under breast, give blessing with right—Fingers extended and joined.
   NOTE.—The lines of the cross should be about nine inches in length.
4. *Dominus vobiscum.*—Hands joined.
5. *Initium sancti Evangelii.*—Left hand on altar—With right thumb make small cross on altar, then on forehead, mouth, and breast, left hand being placed under breast.
   NOTE.—If the Last Gospel is read from the Missal, while right thumb makes the small cross on the book, the left hand rests on the Missal also, and is then placed under the breast.
6. *Et verbum caro.*—Genuflect towards corner of altar—Both hands on altar—Book not kissed at end—Close Missal, with opening towards centre of altar.
7. *De Profundis* (in Ireland only) said standing *in plano*. Prayers after Mass recited kneeling on lowest step, *junctis manibus*; but custom would seem to sanction the holding of the Chalice.

8. Before leaving altar, profound bow to Cross, or genuflection if Blessed Sacrament is reserved—Put on biretta.

9. While unvesting, kiss cross on Stole, Maniple, and Amice.

10. Washing of hands after Mass, though not prescribed by the Rubrics, is commendable.

NOTE.—Orationem "Obsecro te, dulcissime Domine Jesu Christe," post Missam recitantibus Pius Papa X. defectus et culpas in ea persolvenda contractas indulsit.

Appendix

Rubrics of Mass When the Blessed Sacrament Is Exposed

1. On reaching altar, remove biretta—Genuflect on both knees—Profound bow.
2. Place Chalice on altar—Genuflect—Arrange Chalice.
3. Genuflect before going to Epistle side to open Missal.
4. Return to centre—Genuflect before descending altar—Care should be taken not to turn back on Blessed Sacrament while doing so.
5. *In Nomine Patris.*—Genuflect with one knee on lowest step.
6. *Oramus Te Domine.*—Genuflect before saying prayer—Kiss altar—Genuflect.
   NOTE.—When going from centre of altar to either side, kiss altar or perform action prescribed, then genuflect. When returning from either side to centre, first genuflect, then kiss altar, etc.
7. *Dominus vobiscum.*—Kiss altar—Genuflect—Move a little to left—Turn half-way round, so that back may not be towards Blessed Sacrament.

8. *Lavabo inter innocentes.*—Descend *in plano*—Face people while washing and drying fingers—Finish Psalm at Epistle corner.

9. *Orate, fratres.*—Kiss altar—Genuflect—Turn half-way round as at the *Dominus vobiscum*—Turn back same way without completing the circle.

    NOTE.—Server does not ring bell at Sanctus or Consecration.

10. *Corpus Tuum, Domine, quod sumpsi.*—The second ablution is received while standing at the centre, facing Blessed Sacrament as much as possible.

11. *Ite, Missa est.*—Genuflect—Finish the prayer *Placeat Tibi*—Kiss altar—*Benedicat vos Omnipotens Deus* —Genuflect—Turn half-round and give blessing— Without completing circle or genuflecting, go to Gospel corner.

12. Last Gospel—Sign of cross not made on altar.

13. *Verbum caro.*—Genuflect, turning slightly towards Blessed Sacrament.

14. Before leaving altar, genuflect on both knees—Profound bow—Put on biretta—Rise and return to Sacristy.

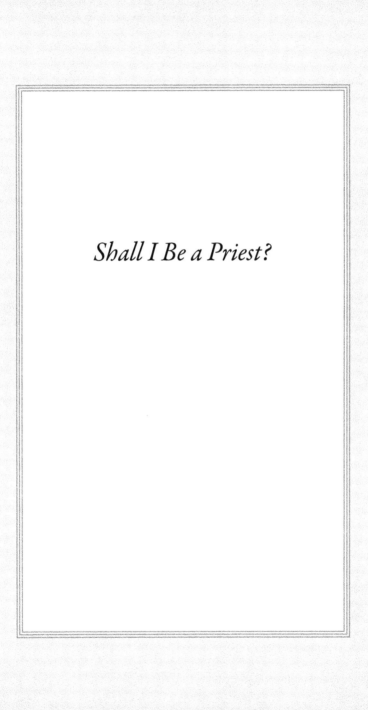

Shall I Be a Priest?

Nihil obstat: Joannes J. Coyne, S. J., *Cens. Tkeol. Dep.*

Imprimatur: Eduardus, *Archiep. Dublinen.,*
Hiberniae Primas
Dublini, die 4 Maii, 1929

Chapter I

"Out of the Mouth of Babes"

"But, mother, is Jesus really there behind that little golden door? Does He never go away? Does He ever get tired? Is He never hungry, or sleepy, and how did He get in there?"

Two big eyes, full of eager questioning, looked up into mother's face, as if fearful that the story of Jesus, dwelling in the Tabernacle, might not be really true.

"Mother, how *did* He get in there?"

The lady smiled with pleasure as she saw how deeply her words had sunk into the heart of her little son, five years of age; and lifting him up in her arms, as she sat before the altar in her castle chapel, she explained to him the mysteries of the Holy Sacrifice and the wonders of the Real Presence.

The child listened eagerly while she told him of those whom God had chosen to be His priests, and of the power given to them alone of bringing the great God down from Heaven to live with us on earth. She told him what a priest could do; how he could wash away every sin and raise the dead soul to life; bring back peace and happiness to the broken-hearted; change the bread and wine at Mass into the living Body of Christ, and bear Him in his hands to be the food of others.

"The holy priest does all that, René, and it is he who puts dear Jesus in the Tabernacle, that you may go to Him and ask Him all you want. He is always glad to see you come to visit Him, He will never grow tired of your company, and, perhaps, if you asked Him, René, He might some day make you also one of His priests, and let you hold Him in your consecrated hands."

Passing the chapel late that night the mother noticed the door half open, and, looking in, saw her baby boy standing on the altar steps. The light of the lamp fell upon his curly head, while, with a look of mingled awe and eager expectation on his face, he stretched out his chubby hands towards the Tabernacle, and whispered:

"Jesus, are You there? Mother says You are; but, Jesus, is it really true?"

With a throbbing heart the mother stood rooted to the spot, as she watched her little René bring a chair and climb upon the altar. "He must be asleep," he murmured, "I'll wake Him up." Tap, tap, tap, upon the Tabernacle door. The child paused, bending forward to hear an answer. Tap, tap— "O Jesus," he cried, with a sob of disappointment in his voice, "I am so sorry You are asleep, for I wanted to ask You to make me a holy priest. I want so much to be a priest that I might hold You in my arms and kiss Your little face as often as I like. Good night, now, dear Jesus; but when You are awake tomorrow I'll come back to you again, for I do want, Oh! so much, to be one day a holy priest."

René was right in his eagerness, for the noblest ambition which can fill the heart of any boy is the desire to be one of God's Holy Priests.

A sweet poet, Wordsworth, once wrote:

A mother is a mother still,
The holiest thing on earth.

Had he known the Catholic priesthood, the sublime dignity and lofty calling of Christ's Anointed, he must have changed his words, since of all God's creatures there can be none more sacred than the priest, whose body, hands and feet, whose lips, eyes, ears, and very soul are "holy to the Lord."

A Priest's Holy Body

In the tabernacles of our churches are kept the Consecrated Vessels for the service of the altar. They are guarded with jealous care, because the anointing with Holy Oils has given them a sacred character; they may never again be put to profane use—their contact with the Precious Body and Blood of Jesus Christ has imparted to them something of His holiness.

A priest's body also is a vessel of holiness, set apart for the service of the altar only, blessed by the imposition of the Bishop's hands, consecrated by the chrism of Ordination, cut off from human love and earthly pleasures by a solemn vow of Chastity. Round that frail but sacred body the Almighty has thrown His protecting arms, and thunders His woes against its violators: "Touch not the Lord's anointed, for I have separated you from other people, that you should be Mine."

"You are," says St. Paul, "a High Priest, holy, innocent, undefiled, separated from sinners and made higher than the heavens."

The Anointed Hands

There is no moment more solemn in the ceremony of Ordination than when the young Levite kneels on the altar steps and stretches forth his hands for their anointing. Across the up-turned palm the Bishop traces a cross with Chrism: "Vouchsafe, O Lord," he prays, "to consecrate and sanctify these hands, that whatever they bless may be blessed, and whatsoever they consecrate may be consecrated and made holy, in the Name of Jesus Christ our Lord. Amen."

With hallowed hands still dripping from the Holy Oils, wrapped in a white linen cloth, symbolic of their purity and their power to bind and loose, the newly-ordained lies prostrate on the ground. The bleeding Stigmata of the saints did not pierce more deeply than the words which he feels are graven in his hands: *"Holy and Sanctified and Consecrated to the Lord."*

Upon them now will rest the Immaculate Body of the Saviour; they will hold the Consecrated Host and break the Bread of Life to thousands of hungering souls. These holy hands will be raised aloft to bless the innocent and absolve the sinner; they will pour the waters of Baptism on the newborn babe, join the sacred bonds of Matrimony and anoint the body of the dying Christian to prepare him for his journey to Eternity. Many a time will they be clasped in prayer and stretched out before the altar throne in mute supplication for the souls of men; their secret power will break the chains of sin, drive back to Hell the spirits of darkness, and ward off from a wicked world the anger of an offended God.

Sacred and holy are the hands of every priest, which can not only bless, absolve, and fortify, but hold and touch the living Body of the Lord.

The Feet of Mercy

"How beautiful upon the mountains," says the Prophet, "are the feet of him who bringeth good tidings, and that preacheth peace."

Such are the feet of God's Messenger of Love, ever ready to hasten, to the bedside of the sick and dying, bringing hope and consolation, pardon and reconciliation to the sinful.

In the morning they "go unto the Altar of God" to offer the daily Sacrifice; they turn from the Tabernacle to the Seat of Mercy, the Confessional; by day and night they hurry through the streets and lanes of our cities, across the valleys and up the mountainside, in heat, and cold, and wet, for souls are ever crying out for the comfort they bear. They are often, like the Master's feet, weary in the pursuit of sinners, seeking the lost sheep of the House of Israel; but the sound of their coming means salvation and the snatching of God's loved children from the fires of Hell.

With these thoughts in her mind, St. Catherine of Siena used to throw herself on her knees and kiss the footprints of the holy feet of priests as they passed her on their mission of peace and mercy.

Lips Bringing Peace

Holy, too, are the lips of the priest, formed to utter words no other man may speak. Seven times a day, with the Psalmist, in the Divine Office, they sing the praises of God; over the bowed head of the repentant sinner they bend to whisper the message of reconciliation: "Go in peace, thy sins are forgiven thee." The dying soul hears them as he sinks into the arms of his Creator, hears them assuring him that all his sins are cancelled, and that he may face his Maker with a brave and trustful hope: "Depart, Christian soul, and may the Lord Jesus meet thee with a smiling and benign countenance," a prayer that God gladly listens to and obeys, for He loves the priest whom he has chosen.

With the morning light these holy, trembling lips, with love and awe, bring down the Lord of all creation upon our altars: "This is My Body—This is My Blood," no longer bread and wine, but the living Body of the great God; a moment more and they are purpled with that life-saving flood which streamed from the open Wounds on Calvary, the Precious Blood of the Saviour of mankind.

Holy lips, indeed, whose mission is to sanctify, to pardon, and to console; whose commands the Lord of Hosts obey, ever making earth brighter and Heaven nearer by the marvellous power given them from on high!

Holy Eyes and Ears

Holy eyes which are closed to earthly things, since they must look so often on the ravishing beauty of the Consecrated Host; eyes which meet the pure gaze of the Hidden God morning after morning during Mass.

Holy ears, the trusted friend of countless souls, to whom are confided secrets none others may hear, into whom are poured the sins, the sorrows, the miseries of the human heart, and thus lighten a little the crushing burden of earth's weary pilgrimage.

The Graven Soul

"Thou art a priest FOR EVER," says the ordaining Bishop, set apart "to offer up gifts and sacrifices for sins" (Heb. v.). As he lays his hands on the bowed head before him, the Eternal Spirit stamps the soul of the priest with His mysterious "Mark" or "Character."

The Jewish priests of the Old Law wore always on their foreheads a silver plate bearing the words: "*Sanctum Domino*—Holy to the Lord"; the Ministers of God's Church carry graven on their souls the Sign of Ordination, which can never be effaced. In the eyes of God and His Heavenly Court he is no longer a man, a sinful child of Adam, but an "*Alter Christus*," another Christ.

"Did I meet an angel and a priest," said St. Francis of Assisi, "I would salute the priest before the angel."

"Thou art a Priest For Ever," is written on his soul. Forever a priest of the Most High with power over the Almighty. For ever, whether a saint on earth or buried in sin, whether glorious in Heaven or burning in Hell, "marked and sealed and signed" as God's most precious treasure which no earthly hand may touch.

Yes, René was right: "Dear Jesus, *I want to be a Holy Priest*," for there is no earthly career more glorious, none more honourable, than the life of those who are called apart to serve the Altar and save souls.

Chapter II

Dignity of the Priesthood

The Elect of God

We turn our thoughts back to the days of Our Lord, to the time when the meek Saviour lived amongst men. Darkness has stretched her mantle over the land, bringing repose and sleep to every living thing, but out on the lonely mountain top a solitary figure kneels in prayer. With bowed head and uplifted hands the Divine Redeemer pours out the "Prayer of God" that His Heavenly Father's blessing may come down upon the work He is about to do.

"And when day was come, He called unto Him His disciples, and He chose twelve of them whom He also named Apostles" (Luke vi.). Lovingly the Saviour must have looked upon the little band, for they were to be His priests, the first ministers of the New Law He had come from Heaven to establish. They were only poor, rough fishermen, but strong with the Divine commission to "teach and baptise," each of the twelve would carry their Master's name to the ends of the earth. To them He would give the power not possessed by the mighty angels, the power "to bind and loose," and change the bread and wine into His own Body and Blood.

"You have not chosen Me," He said, as He saw the shrinking humility of His astonished followers, "You have not chosen Me, but *I have chosen you*" for an honour and dignity unknown in the world before. "I will not now call you servants, but I have called you *Friends*, because all things whatsoever I have heard of My Father, I have made known to you."

"You are the salt of the earth" to season men's lives with the savour of holiness; "You are the light of the world" to lead every straying soul to Me.

Deeply conscious of his own great unworthiness, his faults and failings, many and great though they be, the priest can never forget the loftiness of his calling and that he is *the elect of God*.

"I—the Great God—have chosen you," rings in his ears as the soldiers' bayonets flash to the salute.

"I have chosen you," makes him the welcome guest in every house, gives him the place of honour wherever he goes, while, should he be unmindful of the favours he has received, the un-covered head and reverent bow of those he meets bring home to him that others see in the priest, not a sinful man, but Christ's dear Friend, chosen for a holy work.

St. Martin of Tours was once dining at the table of the Emperor Maximus, in company with all the dignitaries of the court. Filling his goblet with wine, the Emperor presented it to the saint, asking him to bear it to the most distinguished guest in the banqueting-hall. St. Martin rose, and passing by the princes and nobles of the royal suite laid the goblet before his chaplain, exclaiming: "Who is more worthy of this honour than a priest of Jesus Christ?"

"Higher task than that of priesthood," wrote Carlyle, "was allotted to no man! Is it not honour enough therein to spend and to be spent?"

A Priest to Offer Sacrifice

God has ever wished to be worshipped by sacrifice. Cain and Abel offered Him the first-fruits of their flocks, burning the slain victim as a holocaust in His sight. Noah, in gratitude for his deliverance from the Flood, built an altar to the Lord, and thus from age to age the "sweet odour of sacrifice" ascended daily before the throne of God till, with the coming of Christ, was at length fulfilled the prophecy of Malachias: "In every place there is sacrifice, and there is offered to My name a clean oblation"—the adorable Sacrifice of Calvary repeated in the Mass.

This is the great work of the priest: "For every high priest taken from men," says the Apostle, "Is ordained that he may offer up gifts and sacrifices for sins" (Heb. v.).

Sacrifice, that is a solemn, public act of worship, offered in the name and for the welfare of the people is an act of religion which can only be performed by one who has been specially chosen, called and empowered to discharge the office of sacrificer; hence no sacrifice can exist without the priesthood.

"I will go unto the Altar of God," the priest says each morning as he begins his Mass, unto the *Altar of Sacrifice*, for the greatest and most awful of mysteries, to exercise the office of mediator between the Creator and His Creatures. The sins of the world are ever calling to Heaven for vengeance, but the Priest, the man whom God has chosen "to stand between Him and the wicked nation," has the power to turn aside the angry arm of Divine Justice and win pardon and forgiveness for the sinner.

Once while the Israelites were wandering in the desert, a sedition arose against Moses and Aaron, who fled to the Tabernacle to save their lives. "And the Lord said to Moses: Get you out from the midst of this multitude this moment, for I will destroy them." Moses loved his people, stiff-necked and rebellious though they were, and in his hour of need remembered the power of the High Priest, and the honour God ever showed His anointed.

"Take the censer," he said to Aaron, "and put fire in it from the altar, and incense upon it, and go quickly to the people to pray for them: for already wrath is gone out from the Lord, and the plague rageth." (Fourteen thousand seven hundred men were lying dead). "And Aaron, running to the midst of the multitude, which the burning fire was now destroying, offered incense: and standing between the dead and the living, he prayed for the people, and the plague ceased."

Morning after morning, at thousands of altars, other Aarons stand praying with "holy and innocent hands," offering the adorable Sacrifice of Atonement and Propitiation, and once again, as of old, just punishment is averted, and "God does not do the wicked things He said He would do," through love of His priest.

The Ambassador of Christ

An eminent Irish Judge, who hears Mass every day in his own oratory before leaving for the law courts, has been accustomed to show his chaplain every mark of respect and esteem. With his own hands he pours the water on the priest's fingers, holding the towel while he wipes them; he helps him to put on the sacred vestments, serves the Mass himself, and in many other ways strives to impress upon those present the dignity of his guest.

"When I am on circuit," he said once, "I always bear in mind that I am the representative of his Majesty, the King, and I expect and demand that all should remember to show me the honour due to my rank; a priest is the ambassador of Christ, the King of kings, and therefore still more worthy of all the honour we can pay him."

The Ambassador of Christ! A glorious title for anyone to claim! *An Ambassador*, sent by the King of Heaven and Earth to bring His message of "peace and good will" to all men; *a Liberator*, with power to break the chains of Hell and set free the souls held captive by the fetters of sin; *a Consoler*, bearing the balm of consolation to bleeding hearts, bringing back lost happiness by the certainty of forgiveness; *the Representative of God* Himself, raised up to continue His own work: "All power is given to Me in heaven and on earth, go ye, therefore, and teach all nations; whosoever heareth you heareth Me; behold I am with you all days even to the consummation of the world."

Is it any wonder, then, that a certain saint, to whom God had granted the favour of seeing his Angel Guardian in bodily form, noticed on the morning of his Ordination that the Angel, who had always gone before him, now walked behind. The Heavenly Court had seen the marvellous change wrought in the soul by the imposition of hands, though hidden from human eyes.

"I can rule the bodies of men," exclaimed Napoleon, "but the kingship of a priest is over souls; what dignity can equal this!"

Chapter III

Power of the Priesthood

Raised up and chosen by God to be His earthly representative, the guardian and protector of the Flock of Christ, a priest is fitted for his lofty calling by the plenitude of grace poured on him by the sacrament of Holy Orders, and given powers the magnitude of which he can scarcely realise.

The Miracle of the Mass

"Now, there are made many priests," says Thomas à Kempis, "and Christ is offered up in divers places." Custom has made the Holy Sacrifice no longer a wonder, but if Our Lord had not said it, who would have dared to "do this in commemoration of Me"?

To prepare for the first Mass ever offered to God, the Sacrifice of His own beloved Son, many things were needed. Thousands of years of prayer and longing for the promised Redeemer must pass away; the slaying of the Paschal Lamb, with its mysterious rites and ceremonies; the birth of the Virgin Mother, the beautifying of her soul with every virtue to fit her for her glorious mission. Then came the thirty years of hidden life, the betrayal, the mocking and the scourging, till the innocent, bleeding Victim stood ready for the altar of the Cross.

The bread and wine, the consecrated stone, a priest, is all that is needed now, for "at any moment it is in his power to call the Lord of Glory with holy words down upon the earth, to bless Him with his lips, to hold Him in his hands, to receive Him into his mouth, and to distribute Him to the faithful, whilst at the same time the Angels stand about him in reverent awe to honour Him who is sacrificed."

"The power of the priest," exclaims St. Bernardine of Sienna, "surpasses the power of the Blessed Virgin; Mary brought the Son of God only once into this world, the priest can do so daily."

The moment of Consecration comes, the priest's head is bowed as the awful words fall from his lips: "*This is My Body.*" With the swiftness of light, the Lord of Hosts has "leaped down from His throne on high," the substance of the bread has gone, and in his hands, which he has striven to render "holy and undefiled," the Melchisedech of the New Law holds his Creator, Redeemer and Judge. A moment more and by the second words of consecration, "*This is My Blood,*" the Lamb of God lies "mystically slain," for the sacrifice of Calvary and the Altar are the same.

"Whatsoever You Shall Loose upon Earth, Shall Be Loosed also in Heaven"

Not content with humbly submitting Himself to the will of the priest, God has given him the right to sit in judgment on the sins of men and release them from the debt they owe to His offended majesty.

"Go, show yourselves to the priest," He said, "he is My representative on earth, holding in his hands the power of God. No matter what your sins may be, no matter how numerous or repeated times without number, if only he forgives you, so shall I. His authority, his right to forgive is absolute, for I have said to him: '*Whatsoever* you shall bind upon earth, shall be bound also in heaven; and *Whatsoever* you shall loose on earth, shall be loosed also in heaven.'"

Confident in that promise for "God is faithful and cannot deceive," the poor sinner kneels at his confessor's feet. He knows he is not speaking to an ordinary man but to "another Christ" and humbly but trustfully pours into his ear the secrets of his soul. His life has been a sad record of sin and shame. God's love has been scorned, His mercy abused; crime and iniquity heaped up till his sins were more numerous than the sands on the sea-shore.

He has hurled the thunderbolt of destruction at himself; he is stripped of every particle of sanctifying grace and merit; the virtue of charity is gone, Faith and Hope are weakened; the Holy Spirit with His gifts has fled, while before his feet yawns the bottomless pit of hell, from which eternity will not release him. What he has said no one will ever know; sorrow fills his heart, he hears the words: "I absolve thee from thy sins in the name of the Father, Son, and Holy Ghost," and the hideous load of sin drops from his soul forever.

Back hastens the Holy Spirit to His earthly temple, driving out the Powers of Darkness; grace and merit lost by sin are restored; the gates of Hell are closed; and the soul so lately the enemy of God, sealed with the sign of damnation, is once more His child, the heir to the Kingdom of Heaven.

The saints, from time to time, have made the dead body live again, knowing that it must one day crumble to dust, but the miracle of the priest is far greater, raising a dead soul and giving it an eternal life which can never end.

"Oh! Father," exclaimed an officer as he finished his confession, "tell the world there is no happiness to be compared to that which I have found here at your feet. God has given me riches and glory. I have never refused myself any of the false pleasures and joys of passion, but all is nothing to the joy of this day, the happiness of forgiveness."

The Keys of the Kingdom of Heaven

"Knowest thou not," said Pilate, "that I have power to condemn thee, and I have power to release thee?"

Jesus answered: "Thou shouldst not have any power against Me, unless it were given thee from above." Conscious of the great powers bestowed on him at Ordination, the minister of God knows well that they are "given him from above," for the spiritual help of the flock entrusted to his care. To him they bring the little ones that the waters of baptism may make them God's children; he alone can loosen the chains of sin and give back the Wedding Garment of grace. Were he taken from the world, the Mass must cease, Christ would no longer come down from His throne of glory, and the sepulchre of the Tabernacle, where His living Body had lain concealed for ages, would at last be empty.

To him is given the joyous task of preparing the Eucharistic Banquet, of breaking the Bread of Life and feeding with the Food of Angels the souls of those who hunger for love. His hand can bless the marriage bond, cure the sick body by the holy unction, and speed the departing soul, fortified, absolved, and comforted, on its way to Paradise. To him are given even the *"Keys of the Kingdom of Heaven,"* his power reaches out beyond the grave, for, the sentence of "binding or loosing," which he passes in the tribunal of penance, is ratified at the bar of eternal justice above.

How little the world thinks of the priest of God! How little it realises all it owes to him; the chastisement for sin he has warded off, the graces he has won for others, the help he has been to weary hearts, the souls he has saved from Hell. He goes on his way, at times despised and hated, his faults and failings magnified, as if he were not still a man, but the power of God goes with him, the grace of God surrounds him, while love, respect, and reverence follow his footsteps from those who know all they owe to the humble priest, the Ambassador of Christ on earth.

The Power of Priestly Holiness

Armed with the weapons of his sacred calling, the priest is ever an instrument for good; but, strengthened by the power of great personal holiness, he becomes indeed a terror to Hell.

In the little village Ars, near Lyons, lived and died, some fifty years ago, a simple French Curé. He had none of the great gifts which the world looks for in her famous men; so deficient was he in learning, that his Bishop hesitated about ordaining him, and he could call neither talent nor eloquence to his aid. But the Blessed Curé d'Ars possessed a marvellous, secret power over men, the power of personal holiness.

For the last thirty years his life never varied. At midnight, after a broken sleep of only three hours, he entered his confessional, where for eighteen hours he absolved and consoled the hundred thousand pilgrims who annually came to Ars. He revelled in austerities and humiliations, he hungered for prayer, winning souls to God and converting the most hardened sinners by the example of his heroic life as much as by the graces of his sanctity.

Francis Xavier was a saintly priest, too, and thus in ten short years was able to plant the standard of the Cross in fifty-two kingdoms and baptise, with his own hand, over a million pagans.

The famous Cardinal Perronne used to say: "If learning only were needed to refute the Calvinists, I should hope to bring it about; but in order to convert them, one must send them the saintly Francis de Sales."

Holiness in anyone is a mighty force for good, but priestly holiness has a power which charms all men, terrifies Hell, and wins the heart of God.

Chapter IV

A Priest's Work

Saving Souls

"To save souls" is an expression often on the lips of many people, but how few give a thought to all that lies hidden in those words! To save a life is an act of heroism which win the admiration of every man; to save an immortal soul and give it back to God, passes unnoticed in the world.

"Fire! Fire!"

Some years ago a fire broke out in a warehouse of an Irish city with such rapidity that, in a few moments, the whole building was a blazing furnace. The inmates had barely time to save their lives, and a sigh of relief went up when it became known that all had got out safely. But suddenly a cry of horror burst from the crowd and every eye was turned to the top window, where a little boy of ten, with pallid face and terror-stricken eyes, was seen vainly striving to tear down the iron bars of the window. Piteously he stretched forth his hands, screaming for help, while the red tongues of fire, which would soon wrap him round in their fiery embrace, crept higher and higher.

Brave men rushed forward in a mad effort to save the child, but were held back by men not less brave than they, who knew it was madness to enter the building now. "The stairs are burning," they cried, "at any moment the roof may fall in—God help the poor child, his sufferings will soon be over!"

A moment more and a fireman dashed into the burning house, right into the roaring flames. A death-like silence fell on the crowd; strong men's faces turned ghastly white, for none expected to see that hero again. Then, from a thousand throats a mighty cheer burst forth, for there at the window, the boy safely clasped in his arms, stood the gallant fireman. Quickly the escape was run up, and in a few seconds rescued and rescuer stood safely on the ground, just as the blazing roof fell in with a crash.

It was a noble act, and all hearts go out in admiration to the nameless hero; yet, after all, what had he done? He had saved a boy's life, he had given the lad a few more short years to spend in this poor world, which, at its best, is but a Vale of Tears. But a soul? *To save a soul?* What does that mean? It means the rescuing of some poor creature from the never-ending, everlasting pains of Hell, from the flames of the bottomless Pit, and giving him in exchange the unspeakable bliss of Heaven for all eternity. What comparison can there be between the two? If it is a noble and blessed action to save a life, which can only last a few years, what must we think of snatching a soul from endless misery? How content we should feel, if, when we came to die, we could say, "There is one soul in Heaven now who would have been in Hell if it had not been for me." What comfort such a thought would be to a dying man, with what confidence would he go before the Judgment Seat if he could look back and say his life on earth had helped to save even *one immortal soul*.

Who can measure what a holy and zealous priest can do for the salvation of souls? "I think it is no exaggeration to say that every priest is the means of saving at least five thousand souls from being lost eternally in Hell" (Archbishop Lynch of Toronto).

Sometimes God gives him the happiness of absolving a dying sinner, literally snatching him at the last moment from the clutches of the demon, but most of the glorious work is hidden from his eyes. Still he goes bravely on, fighting the never-ending battle for the *hundred and forty thousand persons* who die daily (a million a week), knowing well the infinite value of his morning Mass, the all-saving power of the Precious Blood he offers for sinners, and how easy it is for a priest to win from the Sacred Heart of Christ mercy and forgiveness for the souls He died to save.

The Harvest is Great

Readers of the Life of St. Francis Xavier will remember the agonising cry that broke from his lips as he gazed on the teeming population around him: "Souls, souls! O God, give me souls!" The cry today is: "Priests, priests! send us priests!" for the harvest is waiting, but none to gather it "Send me half a million priests," writes a Jesuit missioner from India, "and I promise to find them abundant work at once." From the Islands comes a despairing appeal: "Bishop Harty has nearly a hundred parishes without priests, Bishop Hendrick sixty more equally destitute. Thousands of pagans are asking for baptism, but there is no one to instruct them."

"My parish in China," writes Father Fraser, "is one hundred miles long by fifty wide. It contains seven hundred and fifty towns, with a population ranging from 500 souls to a quarter of a million each, and to cope with that huge work I have only two priests."

Americans would naturally resent to be placed in the same category as the Heathen Chinese, but, says Archbishop Christie of Oregon, "There are between fifty and sixty million church-less persons in the United States who should be reached by the Catholic Church."

"Most people in England," the Protestant Bishop of Roches-ter stated recently in a public speech, "not only do not worship Almighty God, or believe in Jesus Christ, but they know abso-lutely nothing about Him, probably less than about Mahomet or Confucius…to hundreds of thousands He is practically unknown except as the substance of a hideous oath."

The Bishop of London speaks of his *Pagan diocese*, where not three per cent of the population ever enter a church. There are whole streets within easy walk of Charing Cross, and miles and miles in more obscure places, where the people literally live without God in the world."

Not counting these so-called Christians, at the present mo-ment the world contains nearly a thousand million pagans (1,000,000,000). Placed shoulder to shoulder, they would form a line four hundred thousand (400,000) miles long, or seventeen times round the earth. Passing a given point, in single file, one per second, day and night without ceasing, it would take thirty-one and a half years for the last person in that hideous procession to go by.

Four hundred thousand miles of pagans! Every one of them dear to God, and yet not even knowing His holy Name!

"What Christ did and suffered," says Père Grou, S.J., "He would have endured for the salvation of even a single soul. The salvation of a soul is, then, the price of the Blood of God, the price of the death of God, the price of the greatest sacrifice which Christ could possibly make, which proves that the value of a soul is beyond understanding."

"Could you but see the beauty of a soul, you would be so much enamoured of it that you would do nothing else but ask souls of God" (St. Mary Magdalen de Pazzi).

"Behold, saith the Lord, I will send many *Fishers*, and after this I will send many *Hunters*" (Jer. xvi.). Dear reader, why should you not be one of the "Fishers and Hunters" of men's souls?

Chapter V

Can I Be a Priest?

What Is Necessary?

One of the most momentous acts of the Pontificate of Pius X. was the authoritative settling of the conditions requisite in candidates for Holy Orders.

Spiritual writers had been accustomed to insist on the necessity of a strong interior attraction for the priestly state as a certain sign of the Divine call, and maintained that if this sensible urging of the Holy Spirit, this desire and longing to be a priest of the Most High, were wanting, there could not be any real vocation, and delusion was to be feared.

Great stress was laid on the fact that since a vocation was a free gift of God, an act by which He selects some in preference to others, this choice must be made known *interiorly* to the soul so favoured; without this interior vocation it would be presumption and the height of folly to aspire to such a dignity, recalling the warning of St. Paul: "Neither doth any man take the honour to himself, but he that is *called* by God, as Aaron was" (Heb. V.).

The result of this inaccurate teaching, now shown to be quite contrary to the mind of the Church, was that many a lad, possessing all the qualifications for the making of a splendid priest, was told he had no vocation, because he had no sensible attraction for the life, and even a fear and dread of its obligations.

In 1909 a French priest, Canon Joseph Lahitton, Professor of Dogmatic Theology in the Seminary of Poyanne, in the diocese of Aire and Dax, published his famous book, *La Vocation Sacerdotale*, in which he stated that the traditional view of the Church was that a vocation to the priesthood did not consist in any subjective feeling or inclination ("attrait") for that state, but was manifested by a certain fitness or *idoneity* in the candidate, and that it was the ministers of the Church who really gave the vocation in the calling to Orders. He argued that nothing further was required in the aspirant for a legitimate call from the Bishop than the three conditions laid down by St. Thomas and St. Alphonsus: "probitas vitae, scientia competens et recta intentio," in other words, that there was no need to seek boys with vocations, but rather *candidates for a vocation*, those who by their piety and general fitness gave promise of being worthy of the great gift of vocation bestowed on them at ordination by the Bishop.

A special commission of Cardinals, appointed by Pope Pius X, having examined the question, approved fully of the teaching of Canon Lahitton on sacerdotal vocations, and their judgment was formally sanctioned by the decree of July 2, 1912.

From this decree of the Holy See it is now certain:

(a) That a vocation to the priesthood does not necessarily include any interior inclination of the person or prompting of the Holy Spirit.

(b) That all that is required from aspirants to Ordination is "a right intention, and such fitness of nature and grace, as evidenced in integrity of life and sufficiency of learning, as will give a well-founded hope of his rightly discharging the obligations of the priesthood."

(c) That, given these conditions, a true vocation is unquestionably conferred by the Bishop *at the moment of Ordination.*

Father A. Vermeersch, S.J., of Louvain, in his treatise, *De Religiosis Institutis et Personis*, lays down two signs of a vocation to the priesthood: "One negative, the absence of any impediment (physical deformity, insanity, etc.); the other positive, a firm resolution, with the help of God, to serve Him in the ecclesiastical state." "Is your intention honest and your strength and ability sufficient?" he asks; do you wish to be a priest, not to have an easy, comfortable life, or for the honour and esteem it will bring you, but to do your part in the building up of Christ's Kingdom on earth, convinced that a priest can do far more for God's dishonoured glory, the saving of perishing souls, and the sanctification of his own? If so, a boy may go on to the Altar of God without any doubt whether "he hath been chosen to the sacred ministry and apostolate" (Acts i.), happy and secure in the thought that the Lord hath turned His eyes of love upon him and marked him as His own.

Chapter VI

The Devil's Traps

Knowing well the power of a priest, and how he can spoil the work of Hell for the destruction of souls, the devil, "the enemy of the human race," strives might and main to choke the seeds of a vocation, and stifle the holy aspiration in the hearts of those who hope to stand, one day, at the Altar.

A.—Responsibilities of the Priesthood

Many a generous soul has felt his courage sink and his resolution waver as he thought of the immense responsibilities the priest bears on his shoulders. He knows the tremendous dignity and power conferred on a man by Ordination, and that "Unto whomsoever much is given, of him much shall be required." He pictures to himself the purity of heart and hand, the holiness of life, the bright example of every virtue expected from the guardians of the Holy of Holies; he realises that the care of souls is a heavy burden and a charge not to be rashly undertaken, and that though sacerdotal ordination bestows a vocation on a man, it does not follow that all do well in offering themselves for ordination. "It were better for Judas," said the Lord, "if he had never been born."

It is a clever snare of the evil spirit, which must be met by great trust and confidence in the goodness of Him Who will never refuse His help to those whom He has selected to do His work. "God never calls," says St. Bernardine, "without giving, at the same time, to those whom He calls, sufficient grace for the attainment of the end to which they are called."

B.—Its Dangers

Though the dangers of the priestly calling are not a few, its helps and safeguards are many. Temptations, known only to the Levite himself, spring up in most unexpected quarters. He must walk warily to avoid the pit-falls set for his feet; he must be ready for dangers to soul and body, for "perils in the city, for perils in the wilderness, for perils from false brethren," and, above all, prepared for the envy and hatred of Satan, who "would have him that he might sift him as wheat." But through it all the priest remembers that Christ "has prayed for him that his faith fail not," which braces his courage for the fight, and strong with the grace which comes from the daily Sacrifice, the sevenfold prayer of the Breviary, and his sacred duties, he rests secure, trusting in his Master's promise.

C.—Want of Ability

Not a few are turned away from the service of God by a distrust of their own ability, or the fear of never being able to acquire the learning looked for in a priest. In the acquisition of knowledge the race is not always to the swift; patient, plodding perseverance will do the same work more effectually than the erratic flights of genius. "Experience shows," writes Cardinal Gibbons, "that solid judgment with moderate attainments is far more serviceable to religion than brilliant talents combined with deficiency in practical taste. The occasions for the display of genius are rare; the opportunities for the exercise of mother-wit and discretion occur every hour."

The Church has recently raised to her Altars one who was so wanting in talent and ability for study, that his superiors advised him, several times, to leave the seminary. Even as a priest the Blessed Curé d'Ars often spoke of the labour and pain the preparation of his sermons cost him, calling it the greatest trial of his life; yet no one was more frequently consulted in difficult cases, his answers being full of sound common sense and heavenly wisdom which he found in prayer.

D.—Not Holy Enough

When all else fails, the devil transforms himself into an angel of light, and plays the part of the devotee. He fills the soul of the young aspirant with a sense of his own sinfulness and unworthiness of such an exalted calling, bringing back to his mind the failings of his early days, the times he has yielded to temptation, and how utterly wanting he is, even now, in solid virtue and holiness.

To those who have contracted a habit of sin from which they have not freed themselves, the warning of Almighty God to Moses may be aptly applied: "Come not nigh hither, for the place whereon thou standest is holy ground." The handling of the God of Purity is not for them, until such time, at least, as they have given abundant proof of being "innocent in hands and clean of heart."

But this does not mean that a sinful life in the past need bar a man from Ordination; St. Peter, St. Augustine, and many other holy penitents offended God deeply, yet He did not refuse to number them among His chosen ones. As Cardinal Manning says very truly: "There are two kinds of men who are called by our Lord to be His priests. The first are the innocent. The second are the penitents. The antecedents of these two kinds are widely unlike, but their end is one and the same. They come up to the Altar by paths far apart; but they meet before it in one heart and mind, conformed to the perfection of the great High Priest."

Years of careful training in a seminary, habits of prayer and self-restraint, have crushed down the fierceness of early passion, purifying the soul more and more from the effects of sin, leaving to the graces of Ordination to perfect the work begun by God and fit the weak, unworthy creature for the sublime task of the ministry.

"No one wants you to become a priest if it be not your vocation; but if the priesthood is the crown God has prepared for you, what a loss, and one day what remorse, if you refuse it!" (Rev. J. M. Lelen).

Chapter VII

A Word to Parents

How few parents realise the immense power they possess for moulding the character and shaping the future career of their children. The tiny babe just born to them comes from God's hand with vast possibilities for good and evil; like the young forest tree, its soul may be trained to grow straight and beautiful, or bent and twisted, made horrible and deformed.

Many a priest can look back to his early years and say with gratitude that it was to the watchful care of his parents, to their prayers, their example and holy lives, he owed the happiness of his sacred calling. God held the place of honour in his home; the image of His priestly Heart was ever before his childish eyes, the names of Jesus and Mary were the first he learned to lisp. The stories of God's friends, the Saints, were told him as he lay in his little cot, and mother's hand held his while he said his baby prayers. A few years later, in all the glory of a spotless surplice and soutane, he knelt at the altar to serve his first Mass; was it while he moved among the unseen angels that the great God chose him as His priest?

Thus, step, by step, was he guided by counsel and advice through the perils of youth, till at last his consecrated hands rested on the bowed heads of those who had led him to the Altar of God, giving back to the Creator the child they had received from Him.

Unfortunately, some parents look upon a vocation in the family as a sort of social catastrophe. They may not, perhaps, go so far as directly to crush out the desire for a higher life, which God has planted in their child's heart, but they give it no encouragement. They speak of the advantages of the various professions, the fame to be won as a lawyer or doctor, the glory of a military career, the triumphs of the Diplomatic Service, forgetting the saying of St. Vincent de Paul, "*There is no grander work on earth than to form a priest*," no calling nobler or more honourable than to labour for the salvation of souls as the Ambassador of Christ.

No wonder the hearts of so few young men are fired by this noblest form of ambition, the longing to serve the King of kings, or aspire to the unspeakable dignity of the priesthood.

The great French Cardinal Mermillod, once wrote: "Christian women! Your mother hearts do not burn enough with Divine love that their exhalations should bring forth the heart of a priest. Oh! Ask of God that your families may give sons to the Church, ask Him that you, in your turn, may have the courage of sacrifice, and that from you may be born an apostle: to speak to men about God, to enlighten the world, to serve Him at the altar, is not this, after all, a grand and magnificent destiny?"

Even those parents who have not been blessed with a son, can do much towards helping to find recruits for God's grand army. It is an admitted fact that the multitude of vocations in

France in recent years has been largely due to the wide diffusion of books treating of vocations, and such papers as *The Annals of the Faith*, and *Catholic Missions*. A simple pamphlet put in the hands of a boy may be the means of planting the seed of a vocation in his heart, by making him think what he might one day become.

A wealthy Catholic lady has devoted her life to the noble work of educating poor lads for the priesthood. In a single year she has assisted three hundred and five ecclesiastical students, and in thirty years spent her large fortune in the training of hundreds of priests, many of whom would never have celebrated the Sacred Mysteries but for her generosity and self-sacrifice. In this world, even, she has reaped her reward: "My young Chinese priest, in the first year of his ministry, baptised 1,500 *pagan children*. Most of them, on account of the previous neglect of their parents, died soon after baptism, and went to Heaven. Yet these 1,500 children, snatched from Satan, are only a part of the fruits of his year's labour as a priest."

To give one's child to God and His work may be a sacrifice for a father or mother, but no joy on earth can equal that of parents as they see standing at the altar, the God of Holiness in his hands, the boy who owes his life, his all, to them.

Only a parent can understand the depth of feeling in the following letter, written by a mother on the morning of her son's first Mass.

"Bless God with me, I am now the mother of a priest. When, twenty-four years ago, a son was given me, you remember how I was almost overcome with the intensity of my joy. I beheld him living beside me, stretching forth my hand to the cradle to assure myself that my dream, realised in the flesh, indeed nestled there. How different, how much higher the joy that today fills my soul with emotions never before experienced!

"I am now the Mother of a Priest!"

"The hands, so tiny twenty-four years ago when I kissed them so fondly, are now consecrated hands, destined to hold the Bread of Life.

"That intellect, which through my instrumentality received its light, is now set apart for the service of God.

"That body, which I have nursed and cared for, passing many sleepless nights when disease strove to carry it away, that body is now consecrated. The servant of a priest's soul, it will wear itself out in restoring sinners, teaching the ignorant, dispensing the Lord Himself to all who seek Him.

"That heart, that virgin heart, that touched no other heart save mine, is now sacred.

"When God leads across his path a wandering sinner, how well he will know what words are best to strengthen such a one and bring him back to the truth. Yes, he will go about doing good; he will be a priest after the Heart of Jesus.

"There he stood, tall and serious. There was something glorious in his aspect. I was not far from the sanctuary. Enraptured at what I saw, I dared not move. Presently I saw him kneel before the Sacred Host, and I seemed to hear his thoughts. I could not pray. I could only stammer forth, 'Almighty God, I thank Thee, I thank Thee. This priest was mine. I formed him. His soul was kindled from my soul. He is mine no more. He is Thine. Keep him from the shadow of evil. He is of the earth, earthly; save him from ever offending Thee. Almighty God, I love Thee, I love him, I reverence him; *he is Thy priest.'*

"At Holy Communion, the altar boy saw me coming and said the *Confiteor;* the celebrant turned to me and raised his hand; it was the absolution for his mother. My son! He sobbed, I think; then he took the ciborium and came towards me. What a union! God, His priest, and I.

"Did I pray? I do not know. A strange peace took possession of my soul, which was overflowing with love and thanksgiving. My God and my son! I am almost too happy. There have been sweet days in my life, but this is the happiest of all. For the first time I have a conception of how the endless instant of eternity with God is to be spent. Farewell, I can write no more." (From *Towards the Altar.*)

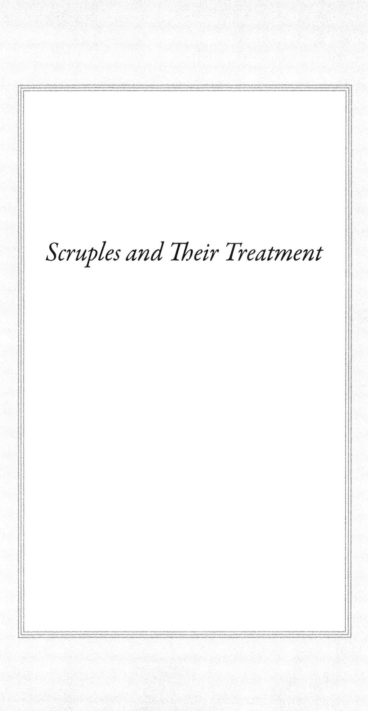

Scruples and Their Treatment

Note

The manuscript copy of this booklet was found among the papers of the late Father William Doyle, S.J. It is partly a translation, partly an adaptation, of *L'Ange Conducteur des Ames Scrupuleuses ou Craintives*, par le R. P. Dupois, S.J. Father Dupois' little book first appeared in 1897, and since then it has gone through sixteen editions. It has been examined and approved of by the Sacred Congregation of the Holy Office, and has, besides, the approbation of many bishops and theologians.

Father Doyle's version has been somewhat reduced in size, and some alterations in it made, and the booklet is now published in the hope that it may be an encouragement and a help to timid and scrupulous souls.

General Considerations

Definition

Scrupulosity, in general, is an ill-founded fear of committing sin.

There are two kinds of scruples: those which affect only the intelligence; those which affect also the sensitive will.

Purely intellectual scruples are really only doubts. They are most frequently met with in straightforward souls, who exercise self-control and are not habitually scrupulous. As soon, therefore, as these souls become morally certain that the act in question is not sinful, the scruple vanishes. This kind of scruple is harmless, and needs no treatment.

The contrary is the case with scruples which affect the inferior part of the soul. From the strong impression produced on the senses these draw a force which resists the mere statement of facts. Such scruples chiefly afflict impressionable souls; in fact, it is their emotional nature which engenders scrupulosity. A practical definition of this kind of scruple would be: an uneasy, ill-founded fear of committing sin, increased by the impressions made on the inferior part of the soul.

An example may help to make clearer these different kinds of scruples. Two persons leave the church on a Sunday morning, fearing that, owing to their many distractions, they have not complied with their obligation of hearing Mass. Having listened to their doubts, their confessor reassures both. However, one only is entirely satisfied. The other soon becomes troubled again, gets nervous, and feels an almost irresistible longing to be quite sure, either by fuller explanation or by hearing another Mass. The first of these persons had only an intellectual scruple, the harmless fear of a loyal soul; the second suffers from nervous fear, which stirs the sensitive part of the soul, and causes a real scruple.

Difficulty in the Treatment of Scruples

A true scruple, being involuntary and spontaneous, the cure will consist, not in preventing it, as this is impossible, but in despising it. But in this lies all the difficulty. How deluded is the scrupulous person who imagines himself cured when he has fully understood his director's decision, and realised the foolishness of his fears! He fancies that it is quite easy to do what he now so clearly sees to be the best. Yet it is only now that the real struggle will begin. For the first time he realises to what lengths the tyranny of his impressions leads him. His feelings become so many iron chains; at every effort made by his confessor's orders, to get free, his hands and feet feel tied down by almost invincible bonds. God will help him, but his cure will be complete only when, by dint of repeated victories, he will have acquired the habit of conquering himself.

God's Plan and the Devil's

God, Who is wisdom and light, wishes man to be guided by his intelligence, and not by the blind feelings of his animal nature. It is, therefore, very far from God's plan that man should regulate his conduct by doubt, which is the enemy of his intelligence. This is so far true, that even God's laws do not bind unless when clear and beyond doubt. The way to heaven is difficult enough for man, on account of the many real obligations which meet him almost at every step. What would it be if he were obliged, under pain of sin, to overcome the obstacle of a thousand doubtful obligations? Such an intolerable state of things would be quite unworthy of the divine wisdom and goodness.

The demon of scrupulosity wishes to upset this merciful design of Providence. In the guidance of man, he tries to replace certainty by doubt, reason by feeling. An angel of darkness himself, he plunges the scrupulous soul into the darkness of ignorance, and imposes on him, as his tyrannical guide, his own wretched doubts, and with fearful results.

Deadly Effects of Scrupulosity

Scrupulosity completely warps the judgment in moral matters. It takes away one's common sense. It places before the eye of conscience a magnifying glass, which enlarges the slightest cause of alarm, and makes a timid soul see a thousand phantom sins, whilst by false reasoning it seeks to persuade it that these are undoubted faults.

Scrupulosity stops all progress in perfection. It is a fundamental truth that we cannot love God unless we believe in His love for us. Scrupulosity completely represses such a belief, and thus paralyses all generous effort. At every moment it creates trouble between the soul and its Creator by pessimistic feelings about the past, and about its present dispositions and actions.

The conclusions foolishly arrived at under the influence of these feelings boldly give the lie to the wise decisions of the confessor, and lead the soul to rebel against his spiritual guidance, and to put itself at the mercy of its enemy. Soon the soul, seriously believing itself to be in a bad way, becomes discouraged, and often begins to commit real sin. Even though sin does not follow from scruples, scrupulosity, nevertheless, retards the soul's progress in several other ways. It represents prayer as full of difficulties. It stops the ears of the poor downcast soul to the consoling voice of the Holy Ghost. It destroys confidence. It prevents the frequentation of the Sacraments, and thus stops their strengthening effects. It almost takes away the power of resisting temptation. It causes discouragement, and may even lead to despair.

Treatment of Scrupulosity

The general rules for the treatment of scruples may be reduced to five: *prayer, vigilance, struggle against depression, obedience, generosity in self-conquest.* On the first three, little need be said; obedience and generosity in self-conquest constitute the basis of the treatment.

First Remedy: Prayer

The precept laid down by our Lord Jesus Christ to pray in temptation is evidently applicable to scruples, which are a great danger even to salvation. Satan would mock at our weakness in our fight with scruples, as Goliath mocked at David, unless we were armed by prayer with the very strength of God. And so prayer, however dry and against the grain, is needed by the soul that is a prey to scruples.

Second Remedy: Vigilance

"Watch ye and pray that ye enter not into temptation" (Matt. 26:41). For a scrupulous soul, what is this holy vigilance recommended by Christ? It is the vigilance of a soldier facing an enemy. To sleep, to throw down one's arms, to neglect precautions, would be serious faults against this warlike vigilance prescribed by our Saviour. How foolish, then, those who think to cure scrupulous souls by recommending them to have a good time of it, to put aside prayer, mortification of the senses, and all care of conscience! Do they consider themselves wiser than Jesus Christ who thus dare to counsel the very opposite to His command?

Third Remedy: Struggle against Depression

If there be anyone who feels the effects of sadness as described by the Wise Man: "The sadness of a man consumes the heart" (Prov. 25:20), it is the poor scrupulous soul. And sadness only increases scrupulosity. The scrupulous, therefore, will do well to have recourse with moderation to innocent amusements, and try to occupy their mind with pleasant thoughts. Above all, such people should strive to keep themselves usefully employed. This is the best antidote to trouble of mind. Does not a trouble, of which we think ten times less, owing to our occupations, become in consequence ten times lighter? No one can pity those who brood over their worries, neglecting the duties of their state, which, whilst giving them necessary distraction, would sanctify their lives and save them much suffering.

Fourth Remedy: Obedience

The two general remedies that yet remain to be discussed, obedience and generosity in self-conquest, are by far the most important.

Without perfect, trustful and blind obedience to an experienced confessor there can be no cure for scrupulosity. This obedience should consist of two things: obedience of action, which carries out exactly all that the director prescribes; and obedience of the intelligence, which believes all that is ordered to be believed.

Obedience of action has for its object the putting into practice the freedom of conscience ordered by the director. To ensure complete cure, this freedom must be fully practised, the least holding back would spoil much, if not everything, since by so acting the scrupulous person would show that he either forgets, or does not believe, that it is God Whom he obeys. Although obedience to one's confessor is necessary for all, it is more indispensable for the scrupulous than for any other.

There are several reasons for this.

1. First of all, because scrupulosity, by affecting the head, takes away one's common sense in matters of conscience. Providence gave the soul common sense as a guide, and now that this is lost, a substitute is sent in the person of the director, a sympathetic and blessed guide, clothed with divine authority, having received a heavenly commission by the words: "He that hears you, hears Me" (Luke 10:16).

2. Not only does scrupulosity deprive man of the enlightened guide given him by his Creator, but at every step it leads him astray in a labyrinth of doubt.

For this reason also obedience is an indispensable guide. For what else can rescue him from this dreadful confusion? Again, when a plant is bent to the ground by the wind, a prop is necessary in order to strengthen it little by little until it is strong enough to withstand the storm. This is the part of a wise director. Not only does he help the soul in every storm, but he teaches it little by little to do without his aid, a result, however, that will be obtained only by an entire and courageous obedience.

But obedience of action must be accompanied and elevated by obedience of the understanding. For of what value, before God, is the servile obedience of the body, if the soul remains in revolt and persists in opposing its own false ideas to those of truth itself? Towards this more noble obedience the efforts of all enlightened directors tend.

In the malady of scruples, the demon, by insinuating wrong ideas, leads his unfortunate victim where he wills. Therefore these ideas must be rectified. They have gradually, under Satan's influence, passed from being mere wrong ideas, through the stage of wrong impressions, on to that of unshaken convictions, and finally have become rules of conduct, over which obedience alone can have any power. It is these errors of the intellect which keep the poor soul away from the Sacraments, and cause it to be guilty of foolish extravagances. But what, it may be asked, are these wrong ideas? The answer can be given in a word: all those by the confessor so considered. Those most generally met with are: "My confessions were bad. My confessor does not understand me, he is mistaken in me, not believing that I could be so wicked. I have never had contrition. I am constantly committing sins against faith, against purity. I blaspheme interiorly. I rash judge, even priests. The oftener I receive Holy Communion, the worse I become," etc. etc. Wrong ideas like these must be given no quarter. It is God Who commands them to be exterminated without mercy, as of old He commanded Saul to destroy the

Amalekites, not even sparing Agag, the king. That is to say, the scrupulous soul must abandon any opinion contrary to that of the director. But once rejected, are such opinions done with? By no means. The Amalekites may feign death, and a guard must be set over apparently dead bodies that may seek to rise again. Above all, there must be a watch for traitors, who may have escaped the carnage, and remain closely concealed in some fold of the obstinate understanding. How may these be discovered? A little watchfulness suffices to detect them. Their presence betrays itself by an equivocation, by an embarrassed silence, or by a want of progress. To the question: "Do you still believe in such or such a theological truth, in such or such a way of looking at your conscience, upon which we were agreed some time ago?" a negative or hesitating answer will be given, or they will say "I dare not act on it." Is not the clinging to one's own opinion at once revealed? Are not the Amalekites discovered?

To sum up this twofold obedience, which is the fourth general remedy of scrupulosity, the scrupulous soul must give the confessor unlimited obedience by believing in, as well as acting on, his decisions and directions. Like St. Peter, this soul has the happiness of listening to Jesus Christ Himself. He is sure that it is really Our Lord Who commands him to walk boldly on the waters by despising foolish fears. Ought he not then to obey the call by casting himself into the sea as the intrepid Apostle did?

Fifth Remedy: Generosity in Self-conquest

Self-conquest consists in persevering acts of self-denial. Vain fears, silly imaginations, all the turmoil and confusion that uncontrolled scrupulosity engenders in the soul, must be resolutely met and opposed at every step. This victory over foolish impressions is also the victory over scrupulosity. But this victory costs much to cowardly and sensual souls; indeed, at first it seems to them impossible. On the other hand, it is easy to souls accustomed to self-denial. St. Aloysius Gonzaga was a striking example of this. Although his conscience was so delicate that he was unusually exposed to the danger of scrupulosity, his heroic mortification had become so habitual and rendered him so docile to his director, that once a thing was shown to be a scruple, it was conquered on the spot. Less heroic and mortified souls will, of course, have greater difficulty in winning a victory. Yet let them not despair. The mountain of difficulties will disappear before perseverance. It is in the nature of impressions to become less vivid, to weaken, when despised, and perseverance in generously ignoring them, and driving them away will make them, in a little time, vanish completely.

Particular Remedies

Besides these general remedies for the cure of scrupulosity thus briefly described, there are some particular and practical rules to be followed, which will be found of great use in freeing the scrupulous soul from its malady. These will now be set out in order.

1. Doubts Must Be Ignored

The scrupulous soul must take no notice of his doubts, that is to say, he must regard as absolutely null and void all doubtful laws, prohibitions or obligations, or any fear of sin, if the motive of the fear be doubtful. More than this. He must consider as doubtful, and consequently as not binding, all laws, obligations, or fears of having sinned, which are not absolute certainties, i.e., as self-evident as that two and two make four. Again, in confession, such a soul must consider himself free to accuse or not accuse himself of mortal sin in any way doubtful. In the same manner he must not impose on himself, as an obligation, the accusation of mortal sins perhaps already confessed. On the contrary, he should boldly set his face against such a confession.

Furthermore, he must abstain from making a confession over again, which, perhaps, was good, or perhaps bad, whatever reason he may have to doubt of its being all right. Let him have no uneasiness in acting thus, since the obligation of making these doubtful confessions over again is in itself doubtful, and consequently not binding.

2. Belief in the Easiness of Forgiveness

The scrupulous soul must believe that all his sins are forgiven immediately each time he makes an act of perfect contrition, or receives absolution, even with imperfect contrition. "But," it may be asked, "how am I to be sure that I have this contrition?" The scrupulous may believe they have the necessary contrition when the act of contrition is made with sincerity. This sincerity is assured when the firm purpose of never sinning again mortally is itself sincere or free from deceit. God so desires the conversion of sinners that He reduces to a minimum the conditions necessary for pardon. He asks only the most ordinary good will, that is to say, the simplest firm purpose of not sinning mortally.

3. Presuming Decisions

When the scrupulous are troubled as to how they should act, they may always presume on the reply which their director probably would give, and they should at once put into practice any relaxation that their director would probably permit. This "probably" should be sufficient for them; because it is God Who, through their confessor, ordains that they should be satisfied, and He will answer for it all. In reality, the trouble of these souls, and their uncertainty as to their director's reply, are merely doubts, and these, as has been seen, are to be put aside and done with at once, by taking the broader path.

4. Lenient View of One's Faults

It is of the greatest importance that the scrupulous should not exaggerate their faults, either to themselves or to their director. The reason for this is obvious. Scrupulosity chiefly consists in seeing sin where there is none, or in exaggerating the malice of actions scarcely reprehensible. The imagination sees through a powerful magnifying glass. The judgment becomes more and more deformed, until the poor soul comes to calumniate itself, telling lies about itself under pretext of greater security. Experience shows that the way in which the scrupulous exaggerate their faults to their confessor under pretext of greater security soon becomes the way in which they look at themselves. One wrong figure will upset a whole calculation; a false weight will not give correct results; but in this case it is worse still, it is the balance itself of the judgment that is rendered useless.

From this exaggeration of faults follows another and a worse evil. The director is completely handicapped. How could even the most skilful doctor cure a patient of whose state he constantly receives false reports? Is it not tempting God for the scrupulous thus to seek to be guided by Him in the person of His minister, whilst they use every means to deceive the latter? By exaggerating their faults, scrupulous persons run the risk of receiving from their confessor discouraging replies, and decisions which are over severe, and which will be to them as so much poison. Denying steadily that the most efficacious remedies prescribed produce any fruit whatever, they will end by causing their director to despair of their cure and by being abandoned by him.

The scrupulous should lessen rather than exaggerate their failings. In this way, little by little, they will come to see them as they are, and the scales of the balance will be set right. Thus, in speaking of their troubles outside confession, they should be on their guard against over-emphasising certain circumstances, which might make their case worse than it really is; and in their sacramental accusation let them not fear to extenuate rather than exaggerate. For why should they fear, when God Himself, by the mouth of their director, wishes them to act thus?

5. Promptitude in Acting on Decisions

How many scrupulous people there are who have a mania for seeking advice, who make the confessor repeat the same thing a hundred times, but who take very little trouble to put his answers into practice? It is necessary, therefore, that the scrupulous act at once on the decisions of their confessor. Something postponed is something not done. Unless they act at once, they forget what has been said, or only imperfectly remember it, or else it becomes a dead letter by delay. It may even happen that if later they decide to obey, they may no longer be able to recall what exactly has been said, and scruples will arise, and they will not dare to act.

6. Broad-minded Interpretation of Advice

Scrupulous persons should take care, when acting under obedience, to interpret the advice of their confessor in the broadest sense. The demon will try to make the path narrow. God bids them widen it. When they are in doubt as to whether the decisions of their confessor apply to such or such a particular case, or if it might be understood in such or such a sense, let them take the broader way. These reservations in obedience—doing only by halves what their confessor ordains, or interpreting his orders in their narrowest sense—come from a want of faith and courage in conquering foolish fancies. Why should one fear to act freely when it is God Who commands?

7. Not to Pile up Questions

Scrupulous souls should avoid filling their memory (or their notes) with question upon question to put to their director. On the contrary, the wise course is to try to forget doubts and worries as soon as they arise. The effort made to remember all these troubles will only serve to root them more firmly. New difficulties will spring from the old ones, and, even whilst seeking advice, the fear of forgetting something so preoccupies the mind as to diminish the attention paid to the confessor. How much of this worry would vanish like smoke, if only scrupulous souls would not keep it alive by useless dwelling upon it!

Confession

As the Sacrament of Penance is the great cure for scrupulosity, it is also the chief object of attack by the enemy. To meet these attacks the following points must be clearly grasped and kept in mind.

The first trouble that oftentimes is suggested by the devil with regard to confession is this: have past confessions been good? Ought they not to be made over again?

How Far Back Should One Examine and Confess

The answer is easy. Without either reflection or hesitation, the scrupulous soul must at once answer firmly: my past confessions were good. There is only one exception to this: when some past confession, clearly and before all examination, is seen to be bad, and this for reasons as clear as that two and two make four. But, it may be objected, suppose these confessions, about which uneasiness is felt, should really have been bad? It does not matter very much. These bad confessions will be forgiven in the confession now about to be made, provided there is sorrow for all sins committed, known and unknown. Therefore, let the scrupulous soul obey God, Who, in the person of the confessor, forbids these former confessions to be repeated, and Who takes everything on Himself.

Examination of Conscience before Confession

To a scrupulous soul examination of conscience is a perfect anthill of anxieties and a real torture. This is true, whether the scrupulous soul is innocent, or has contracted habits of grievous sin, before which last is by no means rare. For the devil can mingle scruples with grave matter, while littleness of mind, joined to a timid and impressionable character, which is the source of scrupulosity, does not exclude vicious inclinations. In both cases the examination of conscience should be as simple as possible.

For the good scrupulous soul, a rapid glance over the past, since the last confession, will be sufficient and best. If grievous sin has, in the interval, been committed, it will thus be immediately perceived. This done, the obligatory examination ends, as the obligation extends to mortal sins alone. The confessor may, indeed, allow two or three minutes extra for the examination of venial or doubtful mortal sins, but the penitent must promise the confessor that he considers this a work of supererogation and in no wise of obligation.

But how is this examination to be simplified for the scrupulous sinner, that is to say, for one who falls more or less often into mortal sin? Briefly as follows.

Having first ascertained the kind of mortal sin or sins into which the penitent usually falls, the confessor will bid him consider this class or classes of sin for a few seconds, and to decide at once the probable number of times these mortal sins have certainly been committed. As has been said, this rapid glance is, for such a soul, the surest intuition of the truth, and the one least subject to perplexities. After this rapid examination on each of the habitual mortal sins, the confessor will allow his scrupulous penitent to examine for a moment as to whether he may have fallen into any other certainly grievous sins. This done, the examination of obligation is finished. If a few minutes be added for examination of venial sins, it would be well, but this is by no means of obligation.

Contrition

There is no forgiveness of sin without sorrow for sin. This sorrow is of two kinds: perfect contrition, which is sorrow for having offended God because He is so good in Himself; simple contrition or attrition, which arises from some less perfect motive than the love of God, such as the fear of hell, the loss of heaven, etc. Perfect contrition is not necessary for the Sacrament of Penance. An act of attrition is sufficient.

As the following questions relating to sorrow for sin often trouble scrupulous souls, they will be here briefly answered.

1. Is it necessary to feel sorrow?

The act of contrition is an act of the will resolved not to sin mortally. It in no way consists, therefore, either in affectionate regret or in tender feelings in the sensitive part of the soul. A dry, but firm and sincere act of the will is all that is necessary for contrition.

2. Is it necessary to have the firm purpose of avoiding all venial sin?

No attention to venial sin is necessary for contrition. Strictly speaking, every mortal sin might be forgiven without the pardon of a single venial sin. To obtain pardon of venial sin there must, of course, be sorrow for them, but venial sins for which we have either contrition or attrition may be forgiven without pardon being granted for those for which we have no sorrow.

3. Should the act of contrition apply to each mortal sin in particular?

No; any act of contrition embracing all one's mortal sins taken together is sufficient.

4. Can contrition be sincere when one is certain of falling back again into particular mortal sins?

However great our weakness or the force of temptation, we are never absolutely certain of falling back into mortal sin. On the contrary, faith teaches that we shall always have grace sufficient to resist, if we so will.

But no matter how sure we may feel that we shall fall back again into sin, our actual sorrow is none the less good, provided that at the present moment our purpose of amendment is sincere. If we are prepared here and now never to commit mortal sin, our will is right, and anything that comes later to turn it in the wrong direction does not interfere with its present proper disposition.

5. When should the act of contrition be made?
The penitent should make his act of contrition during his preparation for confession, since at the moment of absolution a scrupulous soul is usually so troubled that the act of sorrow is not made attentively.

Accusation

The accusation must be made short, for it is here that fancies and scruples are apt to multiply. The rule of despising doubts must be applied in a broad-minded manner, the confessor imposing brevity, obeyed, and the longing for a fuller accusation in order to secure greater security mortified. Let the penitent accuse himself honestly, and tell everything simply as it appears in the mind. Let him not go back on what has been said, even if it is perceived that inadvertently the exact truth has not been told.

According to the Council of Trent and the surest theology, one is only obliged to confess sins which one is certain are mortal, that is to say, the grave guilt of which is as certain as it is that two and two make four. Sins, mortal in themselves, but which are committed in doubt, are not necessary matter for confession. In the same way sins clearly mortal and clearly committed, but probably already confessed, need not be mentioned. Finally, one is not obliged to confess any aggravating circumstances, no matter how great, unless it change the nature of the sin.

Absolution

May a scrupulous soul refuse absolution? Nothing is more diabolical in a scrupulous soul than the refusal of absolution. Absolution is consented to at times, but on condition that the confessor allow this or that caprice. It is thus the demon becomes the "judge" of this most necessary sacrament, for is it not he who excites the imagination of the poor soul, and fills it with terror? He attaches tremendous importance to this prerogative of judge of absolution which is so foolishly given him, because it gives him a ready means of entangling the scrupulous soul still more hopelessly in his nets, besides depriving it of pardon and grace.

Why should absolution be feared when God, by the mouth of His priest, commands its reception, when He asserts its validity, when He takes all the responsibility, and declares that to refuse it is contrary to common sense?

After Confession

A victory is changed into defeat if, by a skilful manoeuvre, the opposing general should succeed in leading the victorious troops to imagine the battle lost. This is what often happens to the scrupulous soul after a really good confession. It is lost if it lend an ear to Satan, who will try to transform into a sacrilege the excellent confession made. In fact, leaving the confessional is for the scrupulous soul like walking into an ambush where the enemy lies waiting. The preparation for confession, the examination of conscience, the accusation, the words exchanged with the confessor, the contrition, the absolution, in short, everything which goes to make up the sacrament becomes a flock of scruples, which Satan stirs into dangerous activity at the least examination imprudently made. There is no foolish longing the evil one does not excite, no false motive he does not suggest, in order to lead the poor soul to examine into the confession just made. A decisive battle is then fought. If the soul remains in peace and decides that his confession was good, he is saved; an absolution received and believed valid through obedience is a long step towards the overthrow of scrupulosity. If, on the contrary, the confession is condemned as "invalid", or at least if the poor soul remain tormented by the thought of sacrilege, the evil will become worse; he will fall into despair, because in his eyes the only efficacious remedy for his trouble, which is confession, has been changed into poison.

Consequently, on leaving the confessional, let the scrupulous soul observe the two following directions:

1. To refrain from any examination under any pretext whatsoever, either as to the confession itself, or any of its accompanying acts, such as preparation, contrition, etc.

2. In spite of the "gravest reasons" he may have for suspecting the validity of his confession, contrition, etc., once he is not as evidently certain as he is that two and two make four, that this sacrament was unworthily received, he must boldly decide, and this without examination, that his confession was entirely good in spite of contrary impressions.

Cure of Scruples by Receiving Holy Communion

When there is question of levelling a newly-made road, the coarse stones are crushed by a steamroller. Such a levelling or crushing in the case of a scrupulous soul is best accomplished by frequent

Communion. Because each Communion means a definite victory over a scrupulous disposition disposed to throw a thousand difficulties in the way; it means a casting aside of vain fears, a gain in trust and confidence in God, a strengthening of the will in whose proper use complete victory must finally lie. Again, the repeated reception of the Blessed Eucharist by scrupulous souls produces other good effects. It gives joy to the heart, and a delightful consciousness of its union with God. This does away with sadness and the false impression that the soul is not right with its Creator, an impression which scruples frequently produce. Lastly, the facility with which Holy Communion is often received is the surest and most consoling sign that scrupulosity is killed forever.

The scrupulous soul, therefore, should receive Holy Communion as often as his confessor directs. Let him obey blindly, treading under foot all uneasiness and uncertainty, however great it may be, of having perhaps sinned mortally since absolution. He must go to the altar rails after making a simple act of contrition, as he has been ordered, without seeking any other confessor. The promptitude of his cure and a delightful peace will soon be the reward of his obedience.

Storm the Forerunner of Lasting Balm

The scrupulous are nearly always inclined to discouragement, and even to despair, in the course of the treatment just explained. "I have been promised solid peace," they say, "as the reward of this painful treatment, but instead of calm it has greatly increased my disquiet of soul." They speak quite truly. The uneasiness and trouble of soul they complain of are inevitable in the beginning of the treatment, and even when it is almost ended. But these storms foretell a lasting calm which will soon follow. A little thought will convince of this, besides explaining the painful process through which the scrupulous soul is passing to peace.

All the treatment to be undergone by the scrupulous person is of a nature to produce at first great agitation. How could it be otherwise? How could the supports, on which his sickly security leant since childhood, be cut away without pain? How could he renounce everything that brought peace, such as it was, without feeling it intensely; for instance, exaggerating faults, repeating the same accusations, keeping away from Holy Communion for greater security, etc.? Besides, Satan is on the watch to make sin of, to turn into horrible acts, the most lawful liberties. The devil knows that all is now at stake; he is conscious that his victim is slipping from his grasp. Feeling that his long tyranny over this poor soul is about to cease, seeing himself driven from a house where he was master so long, is it wonderful that he should shake it to its very foundations, just as he shakes and convulses the body of a possessed person out of which he is driven by an exorcism?

In almost every undertaking, be it human or supernatural, we must, according to the words of the Psalmist: "Sow in tears to reap in joy" (Ps. 125:5). And St. Paul says: "Now all chastisement for the present indeed seems not to bring with it joy but sorrow; but afterwards it will yield to them that are exercised by it the most peaceful fruit of justice" (Heb. 12:2).

The first effect of a serious operation is an increase of pain and discomfort. Now, the treatment of scrupulosity is equivalent to a series of painful amputations. It lops off one by one those foolish safeguards with which the scrupulous soul had surrounded itself, and which had become a kind of second nature to it. Small wonder, therefore, that pain and distress should result.

Yet this suffering which is experienced is the very best sign that the evil malady is being removed and that a cure is being effected. Consequently, instead of losing courage, the penitent should only redouble both efforts and confidence, assured that the treatment is producing lasting effects, effects foreseen and foretold by those who understand the spiritual life.

A Favourite Stratagem of the Evil One

Sometimes scrupulous souls have temptations which the devil uses to trouble timorous consciences, to distract them in prayer, to keep them back at every step; above all, to crush them by the multiplicity of small worries, and so render their lives impossible. Among these temptations are thoughts of blasphemy, despising holy things, desire for the profanation of sacred objects, and even of the Sacred Host, joy in the sorrow of others, wishing the death of others, doubts against faith, evil intentions in innocent actions, evil thoughts about persons to whom one speaks, finally, temptations against the holy purity in souls that hold such things in horror. These diabolical temptations, though harmless since there is no likelihood of their being consented to, nevertheless, hide, when frequent, a dangerous trick. For woe to the soul that sets about examining and analysing these suggestions! That is what the devil desires. Because this imprudent examination will increase and multiply the temptations, will lead the soul into a maze of doubts and perplexities, from which every effort to extricate itself will only entangle it more hopelessly. The sacraments will become impossible, piety intolerable, and in the end conscience will become wholly unstrung, and despair will be the result. Warned, therefore, by his confessor, of the insidiousness and danger of these temptations, yet assured of their harmlessness if rightly handled, the scrupulous penitent should put them from him at once with quiet scorn, and on no pretext whatsoever must he stop to examine them or recall them when once put away.

Four Complications of Scrupulosity

Scrupulosity may become complicated in various ways, a fact which renders cure very difficult. The complications most often met with are the four following, each of which requires patient and careful treatment.

First Complication: Obstinacy

The first and most dangerous complication of scrupulosity is obstinacy, and the refusal to obey the confessor, above all, when this goes so far as absolutely to refuse to receive the Sacraments.

As a scrupulous soul can only be cured by obedience to his confessor, there is little hope for him, if, instead of following the director God has given him, he prefers as guides the demon of scrupulosity and the demon of disobedience, both of whom will lead him to destruction. "Despair," says the Holy Spirit, "of the man who is wise in his own eyes" (Prov.). Is there not much more reason to despair when this so-called "wise" man is the very blindest of the blind, as are scrupulous souls, and yet refuses obstinately to take the hand of the only guide who can save him from the abyss? The best advice to give such a one is to bid him meditate with faith on each of the two parts of the Gospel sentence: "He that heareth you, heareth Me, and he that despiseth you, despiseth Me" (Luke 10:16). Can he doubt that these words spoken by our Lord to His apostles, apply to priests, heirs to their authority over the penitent? He should also ponder on that other saying of the Saviour: "Unless you become as little children (by your docility), you shall not enter into the kingdom of heaven" (Matt. 18:3). With these poor obstinate souls, the confessor must exhaust every resource of his priestly charity, knowing there is question here of saving a soul from utter ruin. But he will be able to gain nothing with unreasonable minds in moments of excitement, which with them are really crises of madness. All that can then be obtained by zeal is that they may return in better dispositions.

Second Complication: Mortal Sins mingled with Scruples

As has been said, mortal sin may not uncommonly be found to accompany and mingle with scruples. They may mingle even in the most varied proportions. This occurs sometimes to such an extent that the confessor asks himself whether he should devote himself most to the cure of scruples or to the eradication of evil habits.

In dealing with scrupulous sinners the confessor must proceed with great caution. He will, first of all, assure himself that mortal sin has been committed, which is not lightly to be admitted in a scrupulous soul, but only after palpable and certain proof. Next he will endeavour, as speedily as possible, to arrive at the number and species of these grave sins, so as to limit the evil, that is to say, to reduce their number and kind to a minimum, in his own mind first of all, and then in the mind of the penitent. It is of the utmost importance that this scrupulous sinner should regard as mortal only this minimum of grave sins. To secure this the confessor will oblige him to disregard doubtful mortal sins. He will tell him there is no danger in acting thus, since even if these doubtful sins were really mortal, they would be effaced by contrition and the Sacraments. To forestall any uneasiness, the confessor should, of his own accord, assure the penitent that he regards the serious sins confessed as really mortal, but that in spite of these grave sins he maintains that his penitent is scrupulous, and that the treatment laid down is necessary.

The confessor will have less hesitation in continuing the treatment, as scrupulous sinners are, as a rule, the most timid in making use of the liberties permitted them.

Third Complication: Repetition of Explanations

If there is one class of scrupulous souls more dreaded by directors than any other it is those who are constantly going back on explanations given, or decisions received, because they appear faulty in their eyes.

A penitent who belongs to this class has one thing to recall, and one thing to do: it is his duty to obey the confessor without adding a single word, once the latter, having listened to the reasons given in favour of repetition, or even when not wishing to hear anything, maintains his previous decision. It is God Who then declares through His minister that He takes everything on Himself. It is He Who bids the penitent to obey in silence. What, therefore, need he fear?

Fourth Complication: Incurable State

The fourth complication of scrupulosity is that which results from the advanced age or defective intelligence of the penitent, or from a persistent cowardice which shrinks from applying the treatment. When one or the other of these obstacles is met with, the complete cure of scrupulosity is almost impossible. All that the director can do is to consider how much of the treatment can be prudently attempted. Usually it will be best to try only to lessen the malady and prescribe palliations, above all, when it is perceived that a full and complete treatment will only upset still further a diseased mind, or an old person, whose deeply ingrained habits and notions are unalterable.

Scrupulous and Dangerous Acts of Virtue

It is no uncommon plan of the demon of scrupulosity to so twist and distort even most praiseworthy acts as to take away liberty in their performance, and to impose as obligatory an act that is purely voluntary. A few examples will explain what is meant.

A person, having deprived himself several times, in a spirit of penance, of sugar in his tea or coffee, feels uneasy if he afterwards takes sugar, believing himself "guilty" of sensuality and infidelity to grace.

Meeting in the street several persons of the opposite sex, the sight of whom might cause me trouble, I have for a long time past imposed on myself the act of self-denial of not looking at them. Now, although my confessor assures me that I may look at them deliberately without shadow of sin, I am afraid to do so, and would believe myself "guilty" of any evil thoughts that might arise from so doing.

In these and a thousand other instances, the devil endeavours to steal away liberty of action, and to impose an obligation where there is none. He presents to the scrupulous soul a puzzling dilemma. If one acts against one's foolish fears and asserts liberty of action, one omits what is more perfect, nay, what seems to be alone allowed. On the other hand, if one submits to the yoke of scrupulosity, many things generally allowed would have to be omitted, and liberty would be ever increasingly restricted. What course, then, should be taken?

The most experienced masters of the spiritual life, when confronted with a case of this kind, give the following advice, the wisdom of which will be appreciated each time it is followed.

The penitent should enquire of his director, if it is not self-evident, whether the act in question is sinful or not. If assured that it is quite lawful, he should resolve:

1. To perform the act about which he is troubled, six, seven or eight times, or as often as may be necessary to acquire the habit of acting freely and stifling foolish remorse.

2. Afterwards to deny himself, by doing what is more perfect, but with the knowledge that the opposite way of acting would cause no uneasiness or scruples.

Without such a resolution, resolutely and perseveringly carried out, the poor anxious soul will remain caught in this dilemma of the devil as in a vice, which tightens more and more. For once the soul allows itself to be thus entrapped, the devil will multiply trouble on trouble, and fill the most indispensable actions with perplexities and difficulties. On the other hand, as experience teaches, once these acts of mortification are done freely under obedience, they are done joyfully and with ease, the spirit of God and the spirit of liberty going always hand in hand. Obedience to the demon is hard; obedience to God is a pleasure.

It may be asked whence arises this dangerous complication of scrupulosity? It comes from the timidity which does not allow the soul to be content with the perfect security given by the confessor's assurance or by common sense, both of which declare that the action in question may be performed without even the shadow of sin. The soul is troubled because it seeks "a greater security" than Providence wishes to grant, that is to say, the security given by reason or the reply of the confessor.

Scruples regarding Holy Purity

As the scruples of pious persons are often concerned with the virtue of purity, many may find it useful and consoling to recall the following.

Mortal Sin not Probable

In order that a mortal sin against purity be committed, it is necessary (as for every mortal sin) that there be at the time and at the same moment full consent and full actual attention to the grave malice of the thought, word or action. In other words, in order to sin mortally, there must be perfect knowledge and full consent, the one clearly perceiving, the other fully accepting, the grave sin. Besides this it is necessary that both acts be simultaneous. Is this what happens in the thoughts or liberties of pious souls against the angelic virtue? Certainly not.

Nearly always they do not realise they are doing wrong; they completely forget their thought or act is sinful, even though a moment before they may have clearly perceived its malice. In all such cases they do not commit sin, since they are not conscious of wrong while thinking or acting. Or they only see the malice of their thought or act in a confused way, and though there may be full consent of will, the fault is no more than venial, since the knowledge of the wrong is imperfect.

Two Principles of Security

Should souls that have been tempted against purity examine whether they have consented? They must not think of doing so. These examinations are imprudent and dangerous, their only result being to upset one's peace of mind, or bring back the temptation with renewed force. Besides they are quite unnecessary, because a scrupulous soul may take for rule the two following principles. Firstly, every time mortal sin is committed, the soul knows it clearly before any examination. Secondly, on the other hand, the soul is certain that mortal sin has not been committed when there is any doubt on the matter.

But, it may be objected, if unhappily in these temptations consent has been given either mortally or venially, is not examination necessary for accusation? No; such examination is neither necessary nor useful; it is even very dangerous, as has been said, since it is likely to renew the temptation. According to the first principle laid down, it is certain that no mortal sin has been commuted, since there is no certainty of it before examination. Besides, even if mortal sin was committed (which is not admitted), or a venial sin, these mortal and venial sins would be blotted out either by the first act of sincere sorrow made, or by the first absolution received.

Bold Affirmation of Victory

The scrupulous soul struggling with the demon of impurity may, relying on the principles of security given above, constantly affirm that it has been victorious. This should be done often and boldly. To do so is of importance for the continuation of victory. For nothing gives such spirit and generosity in the struggle as the secret confidence that one is faithful and united to God. On the other hand, the soul becomes discouraged if it believes, even wrongfully, that it has sinned mortally. It is then that it will give in to the temptation and verify the well-known axiom: "A battle believed to be lost, is a lost battle."

Cut Down Examination and Accusation

Examination and accusation of sins against purity should be reduced to a minimum. Without previous examination, it will be enough for the scrupulous soul, which has been tempted against the holy virtue, to say to the confessor: "Father, I have been tempted against the virtue of purity, will you kindly question me?" An experienced and prudent confessor will at once understand the case after a question or two, and will probably forbid the penitent to examine or accuse himself further in detail, but to be content with a general accusation.

Care of Health

As ill-health or want of certain bodily precautions are oftentimes the source of temptations against purity, the confessor will at times be able to give advice or suggest remedies that will lessen or completely remove the temptation. Theologians agree that those private attentions necessary to health often recommended by doctors are allowable, and are in no way an occasion of mortal sin. It is, therefore, certain the confessor will not forbid them, especially to scrupulous souls. On their side, penitents should disregard or despise any temptation that may arise in the performance of these lawful actions.

Utility of these Temptations

Instead of being discouraged, souls strongly tempted against holy purity should look on themselves as highly privileged. It is a truth of Christianity that God only permits trials for our greater good. The Holy Spirit assures us of this by the mouth of St. Paul: "To them that love God all things (even the vilest temptations) work together unto good" (Rom. 8:28).

This great Apostle, who, in spite of his high sanctity, bore the assaults of the impure spirit, received as consolation from the Holy Spirit these words: "Power (chastity) is made perfect in infirmity (temptation) (2 Cor. 12:9). That is why he boldly adds: "Gladly, therefore, will I glory in my infirmities (temptations), that the power (chastity) of Christ may dwell in me."

Doubtful Security: Unshaken Security

To sum up all that has been said, the scrupulous soul has the choice of two certainties: the one precarious and unstable, the other unshaken and even divine, since it is God Himself Who is its author and guarantees its solidity.

The first is that deceitful security, which the scrupulous soul seeks, by always taking what he considers the surest side, but in reality by obeying his foolish fears and the demon of scrupulosity, which lead him into continual and even greater difficulties.

The second security is that which comes from heaven through his confessor. By following the advice of his director, the scrupulous soul is absolutely sure of not committing sin, because he is certain of thus being guided like a little child by the hand of God, which is one with that of the hand of his confessor. This security is so complete and absolute, that even if the director should be deceived, the obedient soul would still be secure, because even in this case it is God Who is obeyed. It is He Who commands obedience in spite of doubts and fears, and takes upon Himself all the responsibility.

There is no greater security of conscience than obedience to one's confessor, joined to the secret assurance of conscience, attesting that one's contrition is sincere. And this contrition, as already explained, is nothing more than the sincere will of never sinning mortally again.

This security, founded on obedience and true sorrow, is that with which God ordains that man should be content. It is a reasonable security, theologically accurate, truly divine. It is the supreme security. To wish for any other greater would be to seek the impossible, and to cast oneself into the abyss.

Also available from The Cenacle Press at Silverstream Priory

Robert Hugh Benson
The King's Achievement
By What Authority
The Friendship of Christ
Papers of a Pariah
Confessions of a Convert

Blessed Columba
Marmion OSB
Christ the Ideal of the Monk
Christ in His Mysteries
Words of Life On the
Margin of the Missal

Dom Pius De
Hemptinne OSB
A Benedictine Soul: Biography,
Letters, and Spiritual Writings
of Dom Pius De Hemptinne

Dom Hubert
Van Zeller OSB
Letters to A Soul
We Work While the Light
Lasts
The Yoke of Divine Love

Dom Eugene Vandeur OSB
Hail Mary

Maurice Zundel
The Splendour of the Liturgy

Father Ryan T Sliwa
New Nazareth's In Us

Monks of Silverstream Priory
Dawn Tears, Spring Light,
Rood Peace: Poems

cenaclepress.com

www.ingramcontent.com/pod-product-compliance
Lightning Source LLC
Chambersburg PA
CBHW021312100125
20189CB00012B/451